SHOOTING HOOPS AND SKATING LOOPS

Great Inventions in Sports

ALANNAH HEGEDUS & KAITLIN RAINEY

ILLUSTRATED BY BILL SLAVIN

TUNDRA BOOKS

For Paul and his shaggy dog, Frasier
A.H.

For Jean Wheatley and Glen Strathy
K.R.

For Alan
B.S.

Text copyright © 1999 by Alannah Hegedus and Kaitlin Rainey
Illustrations copyright © 1999 by Bill Slavin

Published in Canada by Tundra Books, *McClelland & Stewart Young Readers*,
481 University Avenue, Toronto, Ontario M5G 2E9

Published in the United States by Tundra Books of Northern New York,
P.O. Box 1030, Plattsburgh, New York 12901

Library of Congress Catalog Number: 99-70970

Canadian Cataloguing in Publication Data

Hegedus, Alannah
Shooting hoops and skating loops: great inventions in sports

Includes index.
ISBN 0-88776-453-3

1. Sports – Canada – History – Juvenile literature. 2. Inventions – Canada – History – Juvenile literature.
3. Inventors – Canada – Juvenile literature. I. Rainey, Kaitlin. II. Slavin, Bill. III. Title.

GV585.H43 1999   j796'.0971   C99-930612-X

We acknowledge the support of the Canada Council for the Arts and the Ontario Arts Council
for our publishing program.

We acknowledge the financial support of the Government of Canada through the Book Publishing Industry
Development Program for our publishing activities.

Canadä

Printed and bound in Canada

1 2 3 4 5 6   04 03 02 01 00 99

20108   111/01   £ 17.95   796 HGB

Contents

Chapter 1

Snowshoeing: The Oldest Winter Sport in the New World

Keraronwe checked the laces on his light wooden snowshoes before tying them onto his **moccasins**. Then he tramped over the snow to the starting line. Placing his feet well apart, he took his position. A pistol fired, and Keraronwe burst onto the track, quickly outdistancing all of his competitors. In less than six minutes, he won the mile-long dash. The crowd cheered and spectators jostled to catch a glimpse of the famous snowshoe racer.

Walking on Beaver Tails

Like Keraronwe, all Natives in Canada and the northern states once grew up using snowshoes to travel in winter. The first non-Natives to see the strange footwear were the European explorers. In 1534, Jacques Cartier wrote that he and his men watched Indians walking on snow in shoes that looked like large wooden circles interwoven with leather laces. The French explorers, who kept sinking

into the snow in their regular boots, decided to try the strange-looking shoes. Since the large, flat surface of the snowshoes distributes a person's weight over a large area, it's much easier to stay on top of the snow. The explorers liked them so much that they quickly made them part of their winter equipment. They called their snowshoes beaver tails because that's what they looked like.

Even though all Natives in winter climates used snowshoes, the shape and style differed between nations. There are, however, four basic types: the bearpaw, the Algonquin, the Yukon, and the Ojibwa. The bearpaw gets its name from its rounded oval shape. It does not have a tail, and works well in thick brush and rough terrain. The Algonquin shoe is also called the Maine or Michigan shoe. This teardrop-shaped, all-purpose snowshoe can be found in Maine, Michigan, and the area around Lake Huron. It is longer than the bearpaw, with a short tail and a turned-up toe. The Yukon snowshoe, which is also called the Alaskan, Pickerel, or trail shoe, is longer still, thinner, and has a long tail and a sharply turned-up toe. This snowshoe is useful in mountainous terrain and open country with

Did you know that when skis were new to North America, they were called Norwegian snowshoes? On February 8, 1879, the *Canadian Illustrated News* reported seeing a man cross-country skiing. "The snowshoes are about nine feet long, six inches broad, and have a footboard and toe strap," the article read. "He walks with the aid of a pole."

little bush. The Ojibwa shoe can be as long as seven feet (about 2 meters) and is narrow, with a pointed, up-turned tip and a long, pointed tail. It works well in deep snow and open country.

How Snowshoes Are Made

To make snowshoes, Natives look for straight-grained, hardwood trees without knots (knots prevent the wood from bending easily when the shoe is being shaped). A tree four to six inches (10 to 15 cm) in diameter is best. The builder cuts a log, then splits it into sections about one inch (2.5 cm) thick and three-quarters of an inch (2 cm) wide. These long

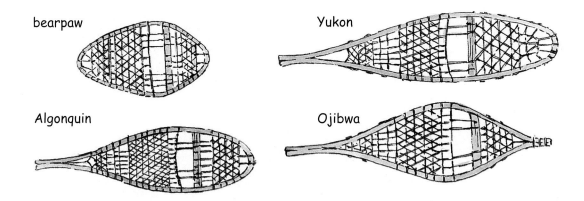

bearpaw

Yukon

Algonquin

Ojibwa

sections are steamed and bent into shape for the snowshoe frames. Crossbars are added at the front and back to strengthen the shoes. Ojibwa shoes are made differently. Instead of steaming and bending one piece of wood for each shoe, Ojibwa Natives use two long strips of wood for each shoe. They lash the wood strips together at the tip and the tail. The advantage of this distinctive shape is that the toe point cuts through deep snow, so no snow piles up on the front of the shoe.

Once the wooden frame is prepared, the snowshoe needs to be laced. Different parts of an animal hide are used to lace different parts of the shoe. For the center, which receives the most weight, Natives use the thick back of the hide. The heel and toe are laced with thinner hide, from the belly and flank. Traditionally, the animal hides used most often were moose, caribou, deer, and cow. An experienced lacer can lace a snowshoe very quickly.

Bindings attach snowshoes to footwear. Natives still use leather or **rawhide**, but manufacturing companies make many different types of bindings in various materials, such as a manufactured material called **neoprene**. No matter what the binding, its basic purpose is to secure the instep and toe to the shoe, while allowing the heel to rise and fall freely. Some bindings buckle up, others lace up. Traditional Native bindings all lace up. As a snowshoer walks, the bound toe lifts and pulls the forward part of the snowshoe. The rest of the shoe slides along the snow's surface. It takes practice to tramp in snowshoes. Snowshoers must keep their feet farther apart than when walking, and swing their feet outward with each step so as not to hit the standing leg with the edges of the shoes or land one snowshoe on top of the other.

Caring for Your Snowshoes

Wooden snowshoes should be varnished before they are worn, and varnished again at the end of each season. When drying snowshoes, keep them away from the heat source so they do not warp. During the winter, they should stay in a garage, porch, or outdoor shed to keep them at the cold outdoor temperatures. After snowshoeing season, the shoes need to be stored in a cool, dry place, out of direct sunlight.

What Were Snowshoes Originally Used For?

For European settlers, snowshoes were a necessity just for winter walking and survival. Fur trappers, woodsmen, hunters, explorers, surveyors, and missionaries would not have been able to perform their jobs without them. Even soldiers wore snowshoes. In 1758, the Battle on Snowshoes was fought between French and British settlers near Lake George, New York, in the Adirondack Mountains. From then on, snowshoes were standard military equipment.

During the summer, settlers were busy farming and building, activities that ceased with the snow's arrival. Leisure time increased during the long winter, but the cold and snow limited activity. Settlers decided to overcome this problem by using the snowshoe for recreation. In 1840, twelve men in Montreal began meeting every Saturday afternoon to "**tramp**" through the snow together on snowshoes. We don't know how people came to use the word *tramp* for a snowshoe hike, but it certainly conveys the sound of shoes crunching on the snow.

The men enjoyed their sport so much that they decided to create a club. In 1843,

the Montreal Snow Shoe Club was born. Following Montreal's lead, many other communities also founded snowshoe clubs. After a tramp, participants gathered to eat, drink, dance, and sing. They also "bounced" new members and guests to welcome them. Snowshoers formed a circle around an outstretched blanket and held on tightly to the edges. The person being bounced climbed onto the blanket and lay still. Then the snowshoers tossed the person in the air three times.

Did you know that track-and-field summer hurdle races were not held until at least ten years after the first 1843 snowshoe steeplechase?

The Birth of a Sport

Members of the Montreal Snow Shoe Club decided that instead of just hiking, they would try racing on snowshoes. They held a one-mile (1.5-km) steeplechase, in which snowshoers raced over high hurdles. This race was so successful that snowshoeing was soon divided into two activities: tramping and racing. In 1852, snowshoe clubs added cross-country racing.

By 1868, snowshoeing was a sport throughout Canada and the northern United States. Clubs organized sprints, distance and hurdle races, cross-country races, and tramps.

Did you know that a pistol was first fired to signal a race's start in 1868? Until then, a start was signaled by a drum tap, a shout, or the drop of a cap.

The Montreal Snow Shoe Club even established the type and order of races at a meet. First, the two-mile (3-km) Indian race was run. It was called this simply because Natives competed in it. Second came the open one-mile (1.5-km) race, which any snowshoer could enter. Next were the hurdles, then the half-mile (0.75-km) boy's race, the one-hundred-yard (90-m) dash, and the garrison (military) or open half-mile (0.75 km). The two-mile (3-km) club race, which was the most prestigious event, was run seventh, and the day closed with the half-mile (0.75-km) dash. During the 1870s, it was considered so important to measure races precisely that clubs hired professional surveyors to make sure the distances were exact!

Snowshoers were proud of their stamina and fortitude. And with good reason: running in snowshoes is no easy feat. Over time, snowshoeing became associated with strength of character, manliness, and independence, as well as being recognized as good exercise.

A Game of Follow-the-Leader

Like the snowshoe races, snowshoe tramps were well-organized affairs. The highest-ranking officer (of the club or military detachment) took the position of leader, and no one was allowed to pass him without his permission. The other trampers followed the leader, often in single file when going through wooded areas. At the end came the **whipper-in**. This man was an experienced snowshoer whose job was to keep everyone together, repair any snowshoes that might break along the tramp, and offer help to anyone who needed it.

In New England community hikes, two whippers-in also helped women and children over fences and through deep snow. Whole families joined these community hikes, during which participants tramped to a secret destination. The group would follow the hike's organizers to a local farm, and the farm family would provide dinner. Only the organizers and the farm family knew the route beforehand, which gave some mystery to the outing.

Although snowshoe clubs shared a uniform (which included a blanket coat with a colorful sash or belt, a toque in the club color, moccasins, and snowshoes), their sport did not have common rules and regulations. So, in 1871, the members of a group of Montreal-area snowshoe clubs held a convention to establish some. They agreed on the size and weight for racing snowshoes, but it was not until 1878 that the first written rules of the sport were published. These were called the Laws of Snow Shoe Racing. Before them, the only written rules were those printed at the bottom of the advertisements for races.

That's No Sport for a Lady

In the 1800s, women and girls wore snowshoes to run errands and do chores, but they were not supposed to take part in tramps. Doctors, educators, and clergy said that snowshoeing was "unladylike" and could damage their delicate bones! At that time, women were even criticized for swinging on swings because men believed that could give them a cold.

In the 1850s, American Amelia Bloomer introduced some wide, loose pants. Women could wear these "bloomers," move freely, and still look dignified. Bloomers finally gave women the freedom to participate in sports, and women at last began to attend snowshoe tramps.

A Sport for the Ages

In 1882, the vice-president of the Montreal Snow Shoe Club had the idea of holding a winter carnival, and his dream became reality in 1883, with the first Montreal Winter Carnival. Carnival-goers saw displays about agriculture and rural life, and enjoyed winter sports competitions, including snowshoe races, toboggan races, speed skating, figure skating, and the first hockey tournament.

The showpiece of the carnival was a huge ice fort with exhibits inside. On the final evening, the snowshoers divided into two groups, the attackers and the defenders of the fort. Each snowshoer carried a lit torch. The defenders took their places inside the fort, while the attackers, who had gathered at nearby Mount Royal, walked by torchlight to the fort. Once they arrived,

a mock battle took place. The moving lights, ice, and shadowy figures created such a beautiful spectacle that the battle became the traditional closing ceremony of the carnival. In some years, there were as many as sixteen hundred snowshoers taking part, making a big, exciting show.

Snowshoeing, the oldest winter sport in the New World, has been regaining its popularity. Most snowshoes sold today are bought for sport and recreation, and Canada and the northern United States now have numerous snowshoe clubs. One of the sport's advantages is that almost anyone, from children to seniors, can snowshoe. All that's needed are warm clothing, flexible footgear, snowshoes, and bindings. Many people find that individual or group tramps over glistening snow, through forests and fields, help them recover a feeling of connection with nature.

Did you know that the Ojibwa celebrated the first snowfall of winter with a snowshoe dance?

Chapter 2

Sailing the Waves in the Canoe and the Kayak

The Canoe

The modern canoe, so popular as a recreational craft on lakes and rivers across North America, is modeled on the birchbark form used by the Aboriginal people of the woodlands. Made from the bark of the white birch tree, also called the paper birch or canoe birch, birchbark canoes could once be found across Canada and the northern United States, from the Great Lakes to the Northwest Territories, from Maine to Alaska. Today's typical canoe is usually based on the type made in the upper Great Lakes region, where legend has it that the mythical Nanabozho, father of the Algonquin tribes, invented the craft thousands of years ago, on Manitoulin Island in Lake Huron.

Across the woodlands, Native tribes made canoes with local variations. The Mi'kmaq designed theirs with a slight peak in the midsection, while the Beothuk of Newfoundland added an even more dramatic peak and an angular bow and stern. Because of the size

and quality of the birch available to them, the Dene of the Northwest could fashion only smaller bark canoes. One type of Dene canoe was similar in shape to the kayak, in fact, with enclosed decking at either end. Meanwhile, on the Pacific Coast of the continent, where large cedars were more plentiful than birch, a sophisticated style of dugout canoe was developed.

What Were Canoes Originally Used For?

European explorers encountered Natives using birchbark canoes as early as the 1500s, and quickly adopted the lightweight crafts for navigating rivers and lakes in their search for a route to the Pacific. Canoes also became an essential part of the fur trade, and could often be seen returning from the bush loaded with pelts destined for markets in France and England. The kind of canoe used for trade was often as long as thirty-five feet (10.5 m) and could carry as much as one ton (1,000 kg).

In 1608, the French explorer Samuel de Champlain observed Natives involved in the fur trade at the mouth of the Saguenay River (in present-day Quebec) and described their canoes as being strong enough to hold the weight of a "hogshead" (a fifty-gallon cask) but light enough for one man to carry, and measuring "eight or nine yards long,

and about a yard and a half wide in the middle." Later, he fought with the Huron, Montagnais, and Algonquin in a successful battle against the Mohawk, after which they returned "with such speed that every day we made twenty-five to thirty leagues in their canoes" (equivalent to about seventy-five to ninety miles, or 120 to 145 km, per day). The Europeans who saw the Native canoe soon left their unwieldy plank boats in favor of it. As there were few roads for traveling through the New World, it became the preferred method of transportation down rivers and lakes.

While the birchbark canoe seemed ideally suited to the woodlands of the eastern part of the continent, it was completely inadequate for the harsh terrain the Scottish explorer Alexander Mackenzie encountered in his 1793 journey across the Rocky Mountains, from the Peace River (in what is now Alberta) to Bella Coola (in present-day British Columbia). His bark canoe required such frequent repairs that he wrote, "At one time I thought of leaving the canoe, and everything it contained, to go overland." When he neared the Pacific, his guides told him about people "who have wooden canoes much larger than ours, in which they go down a river to the sea." Mackenzie later described this canoe, the cedar dugout of the coastal nations, as "forty-five feet long, four feet wide, and three feet and a half in depth. It was painted black and decorated with white figures of fish of different kinds. The gunwale,

fore-and-aft, was inlaid with the teeth of the sea-otter."

How the Birchbark Canoe Was Made

In the early spring, a Native band's master builder would organize the making of enough canoes for the coming summer and fall. This was a community activity that included both men and women, young and old.

The men would collect the needed bark by first making a horizontal cut with an ax high up around the trunk of a birch tree. Another would then be made at the bottom, above the snow line. Next, an incision was made along the length of the tree, from top to bottom, and the bark was carefully lifted away from the wood until the whole piece was free. The roll of bark was placed in water and weighted with stones to keep it from drying out. This whole process was repeated until enough birch bark was gathered to make the canoes that were needed. White cedar or black spruce trees were then felled, split into lengths, and shaped with a traditional crooked knife to make the **gunwales**, the ribs, and the thin slats that would line the canoe.

Meanwhile, the girls and women gathered quantities of spruce roots, which they peeled and used as thread for sewing the bark. They made small bark boxes to collect sap from spruce trees, which were cut to allow the sap to flow. When gathered in quantity,

the sap was boiled together with animal fat, or **tallow**, and was used to seal the seams on the canoe.

Notably, the canoe was built from the outside in, with the bark the first part to be shaped and the ribs the last. A frame, which served as a pattern for the size and shape of the canoe, was constructed using two long strips of wood notched with holes. The strips were lashed together at either end and carefully measured slats of wood were inserted in between to create the boat's shape and determine its length and width. Using this frame as a guide, the builders would place stakes in the sand to form a long trough. This trough would then support the bark that had been gathered earlier. The wooden frame was placed on top of the bark and was weighted with stones to ensure the canoe had the correct shape.

At this point, the women took over the job of sewing and trimming the bark, using an **awl** to punch holes and lengths of roots as sturdy thread. The seams were coated carefully with the mixture of spruce gum and fat to waterproof them. The frame was then raised up so that its long strips of wood formed the gunwales. These were lashed into place by the women. At the pointed ends of the bow and the stern, where the bark from the sides joined together, curved pieces of wood were slipped in to give the craft its distinctive rounded canoe shape.

> Did you know that no nails or pegs were used to make the traditional birchbark canoe?

Next, thin strips of wood were placed lengthwise along the inside of the bark as a lining, and these were held in place by a few wooden ribs. The ribs, which had been softened and bent in hot water and left to dry in their new curved shape, were now wedged into the bottom of the canoe and fitted up under the gunwales. Finally, a slender piece of wood was secured along the top of the gunwales to protect against the rub of the paddles, and the women once again sealed all of the seams with resin.

Did you know that the kayak was usually built for one, but occasionally versions would be constructed for two?

Kayak and Umiak

In the Far North, the Inuit had fewer resources for boatbuilding than their southern neighbors. On the barren Arctic tundra, where only sturdy small plants grow during the short summer, there were no large trees for making birchbark or dugout canoes. The best wood available was shrubbery such as willow, driftwood from the south that washed up along the shores, and some small spruce that grew in areas just north of where the forest ended. There was little trade with southern tribes, who did not welcome the Inuit, so there was no opportunity to barter, or trade, for wood.

The kind of craft that was possible in the North was dictated by the environment and consisted of sealskin or deerskin stretched over a lightweight wooden frame. Eventually, two different styles of skin-covered boats were developed, the umiak and the kayak. The umiak was an open boat that was meant to hold several people, while the kayak was intended for only one. The kayak had a long narrow design, was pointed at either end, and was covered completely except for the cockpit, where the hunter sat.

The umiak had a streamlined shape that made it a fast boat capable of keeping up a good speed for whale hunting. A strong walrus-hide covering protected it from the ice that the boat had to travel through. The frame, which was lashed together with sealskin, allowed the boat to be flexible in heavy seas and gave it enough strength to transport tons of meat back to camp.

The narrow and lightweight kayak was also a fast boat, an observation made by a chronicler from the English explorer Martin Frobisher's 1577 expedition. The Europeans marveled that their smaller boats, equipped with twenty men and oars, could not match the speed of a single kayaker with one double paddle.

In the central Arctic, a fast kayak with a round bottom and a long slender shape was used for hunting swift caribou in the lakes and rivers. This kind of kayak did not need to be big enough to carry the catch home because the dead caribou floated easily and were either towed or allowed to drift to a spot where the women would collect them and begin the butchering.

The kayak used in the eastern Arctic for hunting sea mammals did not require as much speed as the kind used to hunt caribou, but it did have to be able to support the weight of the animals that were hauled on its deck or towed in behind. These kayaks were built wider and with flatter bottoms for increased stability.

Everything about the kayak was engineered to keep water out of the boat. The hunter wore a coat specially designed to fasten snugly around his face, his wrists, and onto the ledge around the cockpit. This ensured that icy water did not enter his clothing or the kayak. In addition, to keep water from dripping up the paddle to the hands, the double paddle was sometimes fitted with leather bands, called **ferrules**, just below the blade. Because of all these special design features, kayakers sometimes appeared to be one with their boat, darting through the waves and rolling over in the water to take a large wave on the bottom of the kayak rather than over the head. Motorized boats eventually took the place of the traditional kayaks, which are now more common in museums than in Arctic waters.

Chapter 3

Lacrosse: The Game of Healing

In 1636, the French missionary Jean de Brébeuf first saw the Huron play a fast-moving ball game. Teams of more than a hundred players ran hard and fast, passing the ball using sticks curved at the end and laced with a mesh net. The field was enormous and the play intense. Among the Iroquois, or Six Nations, the game was called tewaarathon; the Algonquin called it baggataway; and Brébeuf called it *la crosse*.

A Sport for Warriors

Among the North American Natives who originated the game, lacrosse was much more than recreational. It provided training for warriors, who needed to have tremendous physical strength and endurance. The game allowed them to develop "wind," which is the ability to breathe comfortably while running hard. Lacrosse also had spiritual importance. When a tribe member became ill, the medicine man would call a lacrosse match to be played for the person's health. The game was even an honorable way of settling disputes between nations, a tradition that continues to this day.

In the early game, the lacrosse stick was usually three to four feet (1 to 1.25 m) long, with either a round- or oblong-shaped net at

Lacrosse and the Oka Crisis

In Quebec in 1990, plans to turn Mohawk burial lands into a golf course sparked the Oka Crisis, which developed into a series of confrontations between the First Nations, the police, and the military. Age-old divisions between the Native and non-Native communities were also rekindled. To help mend the rifts the crisis had created, Mohawk lacrosse players proposed a league that would include participants from both sides. They found that playing lacrosse could bring about healing and provide a renewed sense of community.

the end. The net was originally made of spruce roots, like those used for sewing the birchbark canoe, and later of deerskin **thongs**. The ball, which was the size of a tennis ball, was made either of wood (sometimes a knot of wood) or of deerskin stuffed with deer hair. The object of the game was to score a goal by hitting a goalpost with the ball or by getting the ball between two posts. These games were played on a large playing field (sometimes the length of five football fields), where teams with a hundred or more players would compete. Some very large matches had up to a thousand players on each team and were held on a playing field several miles long.

> Did you know that some early lacrosse games lasted for days?

Playing the Ancient Game

Rituals were an important part of the preparation for a match. Players fasted prior to the game and spent the night before singing and dancing, accompanied by musicians with drums and rattles. Two rows of women separated the opposing teams and joined in the festivities. After each hour of vigorous dancing, the men, hot from exertion, would plunge into a cold river. This ritual dancing and bathing continued throughout the night. Some bands also practiced scarification, a ceremony in which a medicine man would scratch the skin on a player's calves, thighs, and arms until the blood flowed. Finally, the lacrosse sticks were immersed in water to give them power, and the warriors attached feathers to their hair to make themselves fast, sharp-sighted, and long-winded like the birds. Then, readied for the match, the warriors dressed in a **loincloth** and applied colorful paint to their bodies.

Did you know that very talented players are buried with their lacrosse sticks even today? Some Natives believe that in the afterworld, lacrosse games are played continuously. The Abenaki believe that the Northern Lights actually represent their ancestors playing the game.

As the morning arrived, a crowd of spectators dressed in bright costumes decorated in beadwork and feathers gathered for the game. The women were responsible for holding the items that had been bet on the outcome of the match. The betting was often lavish, with even children wagering their toys. When all was ready, the players on each side were counted and the chief gave a speech to encourage them. The game began with the ball either placed on the ground or thrown in the air at center field. The rush and tumble of the men was matched with the clash of lacrosse sticks. Players were at times theatrical, making dramatic leaps in the air or over the backs of others. Much of the effort was exerted not to capture the ball, but to prevent the person who had it from making progress toward the goal.

When a match was called to heal the sick, a **shaman** would be positioned at the opposing side's goalpost, where he would attempt to control the outcome of the game with what is called sympathetic magic. Natives would use sympathetic magic to affect the course of an event or the behavior of a person by performing actions on items that were meant to represent that event or person. For example, to control a lacrosse game, a shaman would sit behind the goalpost with the hide of a turtle inside a dish. It was believed that this would attract the ball to the goal like a turtle is attracted to water.

Usually, the medicine men also acted as umpires, with their call being decisive, and the old chiefs kept score with small sticks. During the game, women offered refreshments of water and coffee from the sidelines; they were not allowed on the field during the game. Only rarely did lacrosse matches include both women and men. In these matches, women used their hands rather than lacrosse sticks. Boys and girls, however, often played lacrosse together for recreation.

The Siege of Fort Michilimackinac

In 1763, after the British had taken Fort Michilimackinac (in present-day Michigan) from the French, the Natives planned a massacre disguised as a lacrosse match between forty Ojibwa and forty Sauk. The French had developed an effective alliance with these tribes during years of trading, and they both hated the English, who had possession of the fort. The lacrosse game had been timed to coincide with the British soldiers' celebration of the king's birthday and was intended to seem like participation in the festivities. The contest was held outside the fort, on a large field around which the women gathered, placing bets on the game. The carefully planned match proceeded with wildly erratic play, which was designed to draw the soldiers out of the fort to watch. The women positioned themselves near and inside the fort, with weapons hidden in blankets. When the game had been underway for some time, and many of the soldiers had gathered to watch it, the ball was made to fumble and roll into the fort itself. The spectators, thinking this was more of the wild playing they had been watching, did not realize they had been tricked. The lacrosse players rushed after the ball and quickly retrieved their weapons from the women. They proceeded to kill and capture the British soldiers and retake the fort for the French.

The Invention of Modern Lacrosse

The modern game of lacrosse began to take shape in Montreal in 1856, when a number of clubs first formed and met to play tournaments. At that time, there were no standard rules, so before each match participants agreed on what constituted fair play. According to Dr. William George Beers, the inventor of the modern version of lacrosse, these impromptu rules were "broken at the first opportunity."

During this early period, lacrosse had a reputation for being very rough and demanding in the amount of hard running required. The best players favored a very physical game, one with hard checking and brutal play against the opposing team. Dr. Beers wrote that some clubs considered having doctors and ambulances on hand when games were played.

In 1867, Dr. Beers, together with members of the Montreal club, created the first standard set of rules for lacrosse. His goal was to devise a more scientific and systematic form of the game, which would be appealing for the non-Native player. He found that white players of lacrosse had to train hard to achieve the level of skill that seemed to come naturally to the Natives who had grown up with the game. The non-Native players had little chance of competing fairly on the large field of play used in the traditional game because they could not match the wind of the Native players. On the other hand, when lacrosse became a team sport with clearly defined positions, this was a new experience for the Natives, who were used to a more individual style of play.

The modern game emphasized the use of technique and strategy, which are commonly part of team sports. On the smaller field, the goalkeeper required new skills because more action occurred near the goals. In the Native versions, most of the game was spent running and carrying the ball across the massive field. Fast and accurate throwing also grew more important in the new game, which resulted in a modified style of **crosse** that had a heavier stick and tighter webbing. This new stick let players release the ball more efficiently than some earlier versions. While Beers knew that the new rules had changed the game fundamentally, he felt that the strengths of the original game were maintained and even enhanced by what he called science.

The Professional Game

Over the years, Native teams demonstrated the game many times, fostering growing interest among the non-Native spectators, who often became players themselves. In 1867, Mohawk teams even toured Europe, traveling there again in 1876, when they played for Queen Victoria and at the Paris World's Fair. Clubs formed wherever the game had been played.

Soon lacrosse was played across Canada and the United States, with thousands of fans attending games, which were really community events. The crowds at lacrosse matches were sometimes so large that they represented more than a quarter of the local population. Hockey eventually became the

more popular sport, but in the 1910s lacrosse was much more prevalent and its players were better paid. Professional lacrosse continued its growth into the 1920s and was even included in the 1928 Olympics in Amsterdam. In 1932, box lacrosse, or **boxla**, a new version of the game, was developed. Boxla, now more common in some areas than field lacrosse, took advantage of empty hockey rinks and gave them a summertime use. Lacrosse was still so popular that from the 1930s to the 1950s, games were heard regularly on the radio.

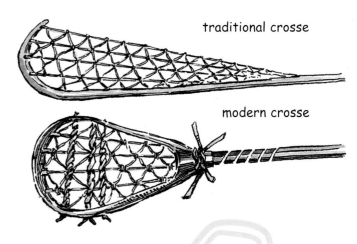

traditional crosse

modern crosse

Did you know that hockey player Wayne Gretzky credits lacrosse with teaching him some of his hockey skills? "I learned how to roll a body check in lacrosse and how to spin away when a guy cross-checks you," he told one of his biographers. "It's carried on to hockey. I've been hit, but I've never been decked."

Chapter 4

Slithering, Sliding Snowsnakes

In northern areas, where winter brings snow and ice, Native North Americans take to the fields and frozen lakes to play the fast, skillful sport of snowsnake. There is no record of when snowsnake was invented, but we do know that the sport is very old, and was passed down by both word and demonstration. Some of the earliest explorers to North America wrote of watching the Natives playing snowsnake. They recorded that it was the main winter game of the Natives, and "the national game" of the Iroquois.

What Is a Snowsnake?

A snowsnake is a kind of wooden spear, carved and painted to look like a snake. The tip is curved, is made larger than the rest of the spear, and has eyes and a mouth painted on it. From this "head," the decorated pole tapers down until it's just a thin tail less than one inch (2.5 cm) in diameter. This tapered shape of the snake allows it to slide over bumps or other irregularities on a prepared track.

It takes much time and effort to make a snowsnake. Traditionally,

---

The Long Road to Acceptance

Unlike some traditional games, such as lacrosse, snowsnake was not adopted by the non-Native community. However, it remained a popular Native game, with teams from Canada and the northern United States competing against each other down through the ages. Recently, snowsnake has enjoyed a small surge in popularity, with non-Natives beginning to learn the game and conservation areas putting on demonstrations and organizing tournaments during the winter.

throwers made their own snakes, but now a retired player known as a **shiner** makes them and brings them to the tournament. Each team will hire its own shiner. He'll be paid a large fee because of his experience, the labor involved, and his secret recipes for waxing and polishing the snowsnakes to make them fast.

Did you know that the head of a snowsnake is larger than the rest of the spear not only so it will resemble an actual snake, but also to give it extra momentum? It's one of the reasons they travel so quickly. The upward curve of the nose also helps the snake slide over bumps more easily.

Each shiner has his own personal method of making snowsnakes, one usually passed down through many generations. First, he looks for young hardwood trees, ideally ones about eight to ten inches (20 to 25 cm) in diameter with a fine grain, to carve into snowsnakes. The shiner may leave the log to dry or soak in oil for up to a year before splitting it and carving the sections into snakes.

Once the snake is carved and shaped, the shiner polishes it with steel wool or a piece of glass to smooth its surface. Then he washes it in clear water, which the wooden snake absorbs, causing it to expand. This forces any splinters or bumps to stand out

so the shiner can see them and sand them down. He repeats this procedure until the snake is smooth all over. Because of the way wood and water react together, the snake expands less and less with each washing and becomes more water-resistant.

Did you know that Iroquois boys use water and snow to make their snow-snakes move faster? They pour water on their snakes and let it freeze, or rub snow on the snake's belly. This reduces the friction of the wooden snowsnake against the track, so it won't slow down as quickly.

The most important thing in a snow-snake is balance. As the shiner makes them, he tests each snake to feel if the head and tail are balanced. Once the snake's balance is right, the shiner pours a melted lead solution through a paper funnel into a hole carved into the nose of the snake. He waits for this to set and harden, then carves and sands the snake's nose into a point like an arrow. The lead solution adds weight to the snake's head and protects it from splitting. After shaping the tip with lead, the shiner prepares the tail. Tails usually have a notch for the thrower's finger, which helps the thrower to grip the snake. Once the snake is fully shaped, the shiner shellacs it so that it repels water. A champion snowsnake takes hundreds of hours and as much as two years to make.

Did you know that some bands threw away their snowsnakes in the springtime? Many Natives believed that their wooden snakes would turn into real snakes when the winter ended.

Preparing the Track

The snow track that the snakes slide along must be built for each competition. On a straight, clear, level area, the builders pile up two to three feet (0.5 to 1 m) of snow in a long, narrow bank. Traditionally, Natives used big pieces of bark to push the snow, but now we have snowplows and shovels. The bank is made highest at the end where the thrower pitches the snake, and then decreases, like a ramp, until it is almost level with the ground. Once the long, narrow mound of snow has been prepared, two players drag a tree trunk about the size of a small birch tree along the snow to create a trough five or six inches (12 to 15 cm) deep.

Once they have packed down the snow and firmed up the track, the builders pour water onto the sides of the groove to freeze it.

Understanding Snow Conditions

Because different snow conditions require different snowsnakes, and conditions change quickly, even during a tournament, a shiner will usually bring twenty to thirty snakes to a competition. The shiner waxes and polishes each snake to match the snow conditions, and helps the thrower choose the best one for each throw. For dry, cold, and fresh snow, the shiner will add shellac so the snake does not absorb moisture. On a wet track, in wet snow, a thrower will use a heavier snowsnake, usually called an oiled snake because it has been soaked in oil and is especially water-repellent. An oiled snake can be used in other situations too, depending on the ability of the shiner to suit it to snow conditions. You can see why the shiner is so important.

Snowsnakes are used repeatedly. After a big tournament, a shiner may scrape off all the shellac and wax and prepare a snowsnake for the next competition. Today, the most popular snowsnakes are the seven-foot (2-m) "long snake" and the three-foot (1-m) "mud cat."

This decreases the friction between the snakes and the track, and makes the snowsnakes slide faster and farther.

The end where the thrower tosses his snake is called the **pitch hole**. The waist-high pitch hole is wide at the mouth, then tapers down to meet the track. In this way, the pitch hole acts as a funnel to guide the snake onto the track. The snow in front of the pitch hole is cleared away to make it easier for throwers to get a running start.

The Rules of the Game

As was the case with early lacrosse and other Native games, snowsnake has no set rules and each nation has its own way of playing. The rules vary from game to game, but are always agreed on beforehand. Nevertheless, each game of snowsnake follows some basic guidelines. Generally, an unlimited number of teams can compete, with each member of each team throwing four times. If the thrower misses the track or his snowsnake jumps off it, he cannot rethrow; he just has to miss that turn. The shiner marks the distance of a throw by putting a stick where the tip of the snake's nose ends up.

Traditionally, teams decide before the game what the winning number of points will be and they will play until that number is met. Games used to last until a team earned ten or twenty points, but now they usually play to four points. That's because it can take a long time for one team to earn ten points. A game can last for hours until one team even earns four points.

The snowsnake that travels the farthest gets one point. If the team with the farthest throw also has the second-farthest, that team gets another point. But if the second-place snowsnake is from another team, then only one point is awarded for that round. If all four of one team's snowsnakes are first, second, third, and fourth, the match is declared a

Did you know that Natives believed the gods would punish them for cheating? Native folklore has many stories that encourage fair play and high moral standards, and show cheaters being penalized. But there is a big difference between cheating and trickery. Tricking and deceiving an opponent are signs of cunning and cleverness, but cheating is dishonest.

Make Your Own Owner Stick

Traditionally, sticks known as owner sticks were used to mark the place where the snowsnake's nose stopped. Owner sticks are usually about two feet (a little more than half a meter) long and are decorated with symbols representing either a family or an individual. These symbols indicate possession, and Natives would write them on their owner sticks just as you might write your name on your lunch box. If a Native's name was Running Deer, for example, his owner stick might bear a piece of rawhide shaped like a running deer and colored if he wanted.

Each person in a tribe had a number of owner sticks, and no one else would take something that was marked with one. A Native might even put his owner stick in front of a pile of twigs gathered to make a fire, or beside food or a drying animal skin.

You can make your own owner stick. To do this, you will need two sticks, one about seven and a half inches (19 cm) long and a quarter of an inch (0.6 cm) thick, and another about two feet (0.5 m) long and half an inch (1.25 cm) thick. You will also need cloth, cardboard, or construction paper to make your design, and yarn, feathers, paint, ribbon, glue, and thread for building and decorating the stick.

To begin, glue or tie the short stick crosswise to the long stick about six inches (15 cm) from the top. Make a symbol that represents you or an aspect of your personality, and attach it to the crosspiece with glue or tie it on. If you're stuck for ideas for your symbol, you can look up a traditional Native one. Next, wrap yarn around the big stick above and below your decoration and stick on feathers, tie on ribbons, or paint your owner stick however you want to decorate and personalize it. Make sure that everything is fastened securely. Then you need to sharpen the bottom of the long stick (you might want to get an adult to help you with this) so you can stick it into the ground easily.

"game out" and that team wins. If there's no game out, then the first individual or team, depending on how the game is being played, to reach the agreed-upon number of points wins.

There are three basic styles of throwing a snowsnake: overhand, underhand, and sidearm. Each thrower needs to decide which method is best for him. The key is to keep the snake balanced properly, and keep a good grip on it. The thrower holds the snake with his throwing hand on the tail. One finger, generally the forefinger, holds the end of the snake, the thumb lays on the top or to one side, and the rest of the fingers press on the side opposite to the thumb. The thrower's other hand is well in front of his throwing hand, lightly touching underneath the head and far enough forward to keep the snake balanced. The thrower runs to the pitch hole, raising his snake to his best release height, removes his forward hand, and then throws his snake as hard as he possibly can and follows through (as in golf, the follow-through helps the snake go farther and stay on the track).

Throwers quickly develop an understanding of the way a snowsnake works as it travels through the air and along the snow. As the snake jets out of the thrower's hand, it travels at speeds of up to 120 miles (195 km) per hour toward the track. Anything moving this quickly can seriously injure a person, so spectators are kept well behind the throwers. In the past, there have been accidents when a snowsnake jumped the track, or missed it altogether, and pierced right through a spectator's boot! Once the snowsnake reaches the track, it can slide for up to a mile (1.5 km). Some throwers can even send a snake as far as two miles (3 km).

Because it's such a technical sport, with players having to concentrate on their speed, balance, and throwing position, among other things, you might think that snowsnake would be a quiet game. But it is *noisy!* As in any good sport, spectators and team members yell, shout, and cheer for their teammates, and loudly boo and jeer their opponents.

Chapter 5

Hockey: The Fastest Sport on Ice

On a winter afternoon in 1886, a group of men sat around a table in Montreal discussing ice hockey. They had just formed the Amateur Hockey Association of Canada. As they discussed, argued about, and agreed on rules and regulations for their new sport, one member said that he hoped it would be played as much in winter as lacrosse was in the summer. Little did they know that hockey would become more popular than they ever dreamed, with teams playing internationally for world championships and Olympic medals.

snowy Canadian winters put an end to games on grassy fields, and players moved onto the frozen surfaces of lakes and ponds. Adding skates made moving on ice easier and faster, and allowed the sport of ice hockey to develop. In all, the path from an informal schoolboy game to a team sport with formal rules took about seventy years.

The Origins of Hockey

Ball and stick games have been played all over the world for centuries, and immigrants to the New World brought their games with them. The Scots played shinty or **shinny**, the English played cricket and **bandy**, and the Irish played **hurley**, all of which were precursors to hockey. However, the long, cold,

The Native Game of Oochamkunutk

Natives also played a game on ice, with bent sticks and a painted or carved wooden ball that they tried to send through an opposing team's goal. Ten men played on each side, and could touch the ball with their sticks or feet but not their hands. Players body-checked, but could not hit other players over the head. This stick-and-ball game was called Oochamkunutk, and Natives played it with and without wooden or bone skates attached to their moccasins.

Because Native culture tended to be passed down orally, instead of in written form, it is difficult to determine the precise timing of historical events. Although early settlers wrote about watching the Mi'kmaq Indians play Oochamkunutk, we do not know for certain whether the Mi'kmaq used skates first, or adopted them after seeing the white settlers playing on the ice.

Hockey's origins have been shrouded in misinformation because Montreal and Halifax each claim that their city was the "birthplace" of the sport. However, the first written report of skating with sticks in an attempt to send a ball through a goal comes from early settlers in the Maritimes.

In fact, Nova Scotia lakes and ponds supported many ice games. Two stones, frozen to the ice a few feet apart, made a goal at each end. The more players skating on the ice, the farther apart the goals were set. One person guarded the goal, while any number of players chased an object around the ice with their sticks. Instead of a rubber puck, they chased after a knot of wood, a ball, a slice from a tree branch, or even frozen horse dung. Before the game, the teams agreed on the number of goals (called games) it would take to win. It was just as exciting to score then as it is today – the triumphant player yelled and cheered and the team whooped and congratulated each other.

Since most of the immigrants in the area were Irish, this game was usually called hurley-on-ice and the sticks were hurleys. In other parts of North America, the game was called break-shins because players would whack each other against the shins with their sticks. This is also where the name shinny is supposed to have come from.

What's in a Name?

No one is sure how the game came to be called hockey, but there are theories about it. One is that hockey comes from the French word *hoquet*, for the shape of a shepherd's crook, which the hockey stick resembled. Another claims that the game is named after Colonel Hockey, who was stationed at Fort Edward, Nova Scotia, and ordered his troops to play hurley-on-ice in the winter to keep them in shape. Although military records do show a Col. John Hockey as having been at Fort Edward, we may never know for sure how the sport got its name.

The Start of Organized Hockey

One young Nova Scotian of the 1850s would grow up to play an important role in hockey's development. He was James George Aylwin Creighton, known to his friends as J.G.A.C. In 1872, J.G.A.C. moved to Montreal from Halifax to work as a railroad engineer. Already an athletic footballer and accomplished figure skater, he joined both the Montreal Football Club and the Victoria Skating Rink. Because of hockey's speed and skill level, J.G.A.C. thought it would be a great sport to keep his fellow footballers in shape during the winter off-season. So he sent off to Halifax for Mi'kmaq hockey sticks, which were considered the best, and set about teaching the game to his friends. It is largely thanks to J.G.A.C. that Nova Scotia gets credit for both the idea of ice hockey and the name of the game.

Did you know that before the invention of sideboards and protective glass, both pucks and players flew into the stands? Sometimes fans held on to an opposing team member to give their team a few seconds' advantage while the player struggled to get back on the ice.

When Did Women Start Playing Hockey?

Women and girls have been playing hockey since the 1800s. At first, they played in sweaters and long skirts. Imagine chasing a puck with lengths of material billowing around your legs! By 1918, knee-length bloomers had replaced the skirts, but women could not wear hockey pants until the 1920s.

During hockey's early years, doctors, educators, and members of the clergy all considered the sport to be "bad" for women. Some husbands even stopped their wives from playing. Now we know better, of course. Today countries around the world have women's hockey teams, and the sport became an official part of the Olympics in 1998.

Although women's hockey is a fast-paced, technically exciting sport, it is less rough than the men's version. Body-checking, for instance, is not allowed in women's hockey. In fact, since hockey's earliest beginnings, women have been more conscious of playing the sport safely. The chest protectors that male goalies wear today, for example, were invented by the mothers of female hockey players in the Canadian Maritimes. They sewed the pads from unbleached cotton and stuffed them with sawdust so their daughters would not be hurt by flying pucks.

Hockey changed in Montreal, though. For example, J.G.A.C. and his friends decided that it would be fun to play on indoor rinks, which were usually reserved for pleasure skaters and figure skaters. But J.G.A.C. belonged to the Victoria Skating Rink, and gained permission to use the rink to play a hockey game on March 3, 1875. This game is historic for two reasons: first, it is the earliest recorded indoor hockey game anywhere, and is often named as the start of organized hockey; and second, items from this Montreal game became part of the modern game that we recognize today. Instead of freezing rocks to the ice to mark the goal, for instance, players set up posts about eight feet (2.5 m) apart. These posts were parallel to the end of the rink instead of to the sides, as they were in the early game. The Montreal game also added one referee and two goal judges, as in lacrosse.

Did you know that the referee Fred C. Waghorne changed the face-off in 1914? Until then, the referee had always placed the puck on the ice between the players' stick blades. Waghorne was the first to drop the puck — which was a lot safer! He also began blowing a whistle to stop play. Before that, referees rang handbells that they carried throughout the game.

Keep Your Eye on the Puck

Often when people played hockey, they chased a ball across the ice. But balls bounce and this makes them harder to control than a flat object. A story about the puck's invention claims that during a game, a hard shot sent the ball flying through the air and out an arena window. The irate rink manager grabbed the ball, pulled out a knife, sliced off the top and bottom of the rubber ball, and threw it back into the game. This is unlikely, although it makes a great tale.

Reports tell of Natives and early settlers using slices of tree limbs as pucks in Nova Scotia, and at the March 3, 1875, game in Montreal, players used "a flat circular piece of wood" because it would slide well on the ice. It also would not bounce into the spectators, who stood on a platform eight inches (20 cm) above the rink to watch, with no boards to protect them.

At this point in hockey's evolution, games still ended when a team scored an agreed-upon number of goals, usually three. The historic Montreal game was meant to stop at three goals, but it ended with a score of two to one. Like many hockey games since, the one in Montreal finished in a fight. Players and spectators entered the fray, players became injured, benches were broken, and female spectators ran out of the building. J.G.A.C. was not in the fight, but he was the captain of the winning team.

The Rules of the Game

Although it ended in a fight, the game was a hit. News of the exciting sport spread, and by 1890 there were hockey teams across Canada and in the northeastern United States. But in those days people did not communicate easily across long distances, so each area played hockey according to its own rules. In the early 1880s, the secretary of Montreal's Victoria Skating Club wrote to dozens of cities, searching for written hockey rules. Since each city's teams just played other teams from the same area, and everyone knew the rules, no club had written them down. This was a problem. Montreal was planning a winter carnival and the city wanted to have a hockey tournament as one of the attractions. But how could teams play each other if they did not all play by the same rules? A committee decided to establish some. For the carnival, each team would have seven players on a side. This seventh player was a "rover" who switched between offense and defense during the game. Also, instead of ending when an agreed-upon number of goals was scored, the game would consist of two periods of thirty minutes each, with a ten-minute intermission. The team that scored the most goals in this fixed time period would win the game.

By 1886, hockey's popularity had grown, and representatives from the newly formed Amateur Hockey Association of Canada produced the first formal set of hockey rules, known as the Montreal rules. The game time remained two periods of thirty minutes each, divided by a ten-minute intermission, as it had been at the carnival. Players could now play the puck when it passed behind the goal; before, play ended if the puck crossed the goal line. However, the puck now had to enter the goal from the front to score. (Because there were no goal nets yet, goals had been allowed no matter what angle the puck came from to get between the posts.) Sticks would have a maximum width of three inches (7.5 cm), but players could choose a suitable length. The puck would be made of vulcanized rubber, and would be one inch (2.5 cm) thick and three inches (7.5 cm) in diameter. Goalposts would sit six feet (1.8 m) apart, parallel to the end of the rink, and stand four feet (1.2 m) high. The goalie had to stand throughout the game – he could not kneel, lie down on the ice, sit, or sprawl to save the puck from passing through the posts. Players could not pass the puck forward. Each side would have seven players: one goaltender, two defensemen,

three forwards, and one rover. Substitutions could be made only if a player was injured; otherwise, players remained on the ice for the whole game.

Soon, teams from everywhere west of the Maritimes adopted these rules, which is why Montreal also gets credit for inventing hockey. In Montreal, the game that began in Nova Scotia was organized into the sport that we recognize today, even though the rules have continued to evolve.

Did you know that television led to painted ice? When television was first invented, and was available only in black and white, viewers found it difficult to see the puck against the clear ice surface — and sometimes so did the camera crew.
To make the black puck stand out better, the surface of the ice was painted white.

Jacques Plante and the Goalie Mask

Montreal Canadiens goalie Jacques Plante developed and popularized the goalie mask. Plante suffered from sinusitis, so he routinely protected his face with a mask during practices. His coach forbade him from wearing it in a game because he believed Plante would play harder if he had to protect his face as well as the goal.

But on November 1, 1959, a puck tore off Plante's nose during a game. A doctor stitched it back on, but Plante said he would return to the ice only if he could wear his mask. His coach agreed, the Canadiens won, and Plante kept wearing a mask.

Plante believed that all goalies needed this protection. After he retired from playing hockey, he manufactured goalie masks, which became standard equipment thanks to him. The seven goalie masks that Plante wore during his career are on display in the Hockey Hall of Fame.

Lord Stanley's Cup

In 1888, Lord Stanley of Preston was appointed to serve as Canada's governor-general. Lord Stanley, Lady Stanley, and their eight sons and two daughters all enjoyed hockey. Lord Stanley even had a rink made on the grounds of his official residence, Rideau Hall in Ottawa, and the whole family played – even on Sunday sometimes, which was considered sinful in Victorian times. In fact, Lord Stanley loved hockey so much that he decided to donate a trophy to be awarded to the championship Canadian hockey club. While in England, one of his aides purchased a silver-plated rose bowl for less than fifty dollars. The bowl was donated in 1893, and was called the Dominion Challenge Trophy. For years, any team could challenge the cup holders at any time during the season, and the winner of that game was awarded the trophy.

Did you know that in 1903, there were so many challenges for the Stanley Cup that the rules were changed? From then on, the Stanley Cup could be played for only at the end of the hockey season.

When the Stanley Cup was first presented, it was just a small rose bowl with a band of silver underneath for engraving the names of the winning team's players. Now it stands several feet high because of all the bands that have been added to accommodate the names

of winners over the years, and it is the oldest and most sought-after team trophy in North America. Unfortunately, Lord Stanley never got to see his cup awarded; his term of office ended and he returned to England in May 1893.

Who Invented Baseball?

Like hockey's, baseball's origins are disputed and have been claimed by a number of different nations. Most people now agree, however, that the sport evolved from rounders, an English children's game in which members of one team take a turn at bat while members of another team position themselves in the field and try to get the runners out as they dash around bases. In North America, rounders was renamed base ball, and it was a favorite pastime of both children and adults. By the 1830s, four different versions existed: the Canadian game, the Massachusetts game, the New York game, and the Philadelphia game.

On June 4, 1838, in Beachville (in what is now Ontario), the first recorded Canadian game took place. In this version, there were eleven players on each team and all eleven had to get "out" before the inning was considered complete and the teams could change positions. There was no designated strike zone. The "knocker" (batter) could let any number of pitches pass while he waited for one he wanted to swing at with his wooden "club" (bat). There were five bases on the field. As a player ran around them, the other team would try to get him out by hitting him with the ball while he was between bases. This was known as soaking, or plugging, a runner.

In 1845, New Yorker Alexander Cartwright took rules from each of the four different types of base ball and added a few of his own. His new version became the basis for the nine-players-per-side, three-outs-per-inning game we recognize today. Cartwright's version quickly spread and the others soon disappeared.

A set of standard rules meant that Canadian and American teams could play each other easily, and the first international championship was held in 1864. Soon team owners in both countries were routinely importing players from across the border. By 1900, baseball was the most popular summer sport on the continent.

In the late 1800s, Americans began to consider baseball their national sport. Because some people didn't want to believe the game had foreign roots, they set up a commission to prove it had its origins in the United States. The commission declared that Abner Doubleday had invented the game in a Cooperstown, New York, schoolyard in 1838, even though there was no evidence that this was so. And since Doubleday had died in 1893, he wasn't around to disagree. The story first appeared in newspapers in 1907, and was quickly accepted as fact. The National Baseball Hall of Fame was even built in Cooperstown, although numerous baseball historians offered evidence of the sport's English origins. The idea that Abner Doubleday invented baseball is so enduring that people still believe it today.

Chapter 6

Ice Skates Take a Turn for the Better

John Forbes and the Acme Skate

Today we buy skates that come with their own boots, but in the early 1800s skates were made to be strapped onto ordinary winter boots. These skates were made from blocks of wood that were shaped to be longer and narrower than the foot of the skater. A bar of steel was prepared by a blacksmith and inserted into a groove on the bottom of the wood. A skater screwed the finished skate onto a boot, first using a **gimlet** to punch a hole into the heel. Straps of leather and sometimes ropes were used to hold the skates in place. This type of skate was called a stock skate.

Did you know that the first skate blades were made from the rib bones of animals?

The difficulty with stock skates was that active skating would loosen them, and the skater would then need to stop and tighten the fastenings. In cold weather, the leather straps would get stiff and were a nuisance to adjust. Sometimes a skate came right off during skating or a sudden stop made the wood split apart. The very design of the stock skate limited the kind of skating that people could do.

Inventing the Acme Skate

In the 1860s, John Forbes was selling stock skates for the Starr Manufacturing Company in Dartmouth, Nova Scotia, and he often heard people's complaints about them. In 1863, he and his assistant, Thomas Bateman, began to work on a design for a sturdy all-metal, self-fastening skate. The result was the Acme Club Skate. Also called a spring skate, the Acme skate did not require leather straps to attach it to a boot. Instead, it clamped into

stock skate

Acme skate

place with a lever that adjusted it to any size of boot. The Starr Manufacturing Company began manufacturing the skate in 1865, and was soon selling it all around the world.

The Acme skate quickly proved popular. It was affordable and easy to attach securely to a boot, which meant people could make turns quickly and not lose a skate. Because it was sturdy enough to stand up to faster and more demanding skating, it changed the face of both figure skating and hockey. In fact, by making a lot of good-quality skates available at reasonable prices, Forbes helped boost the development of the new game of hockey.

The rapid growth of hockey created a market not only for skates, but also for hockey sticks. The demand was more than could be met by the Mi'kmaq carvers who traditionally made the sticks. Around 1900, Starr Manufacturing patented the MicMac, a hockey stick that was made from yellow birch and was named to honor the Native craftsmen.

Did you know that the elaborately curved "turn-overs" at the front of early skates made it easier to glide over bumpy ice?

The Development of the Skating Boot

With the success of the Acme skate, Starr Manufacturing was soon producing several other kinds of skates, and by 1900 had introduced a lighter skate called a tube skate. The tube skate was made of tubular steel and was designed to be screwed onto a skating boot, which by this time had become an important part of a skater's equipment. The boots were specially designed for skating and were made with extra support for the ankles. People would buy the boots and skates separately and screw them together at home. Hockey skates for goalies were made with a special feature called a puck stop, which was a triangular extension that stopped a puck from passing through the space between the boot and the skate.

Did you know that skating was probably first used as a form of transportation in Scandinavia two thousand years ago?

Advertising from the period featured the "Star Skater," wearing his Starr skates and holding a MicMac hockey stick. His image also appeared on arena programs.

The Starr Manufacturing Company was very successful, selling its skates in Canada, the U.S., Britain, France, Germany, Norway, Russia, and China. In 1873, at its peak, the company had 250 employees. Over the years, Starr Manufacturing produced eleven million pairs of skates, and continued making them until 1938, more than seventy-five years after Forbes first invented the Acme skate.

James A. Whelpley and the Long Reach Skate

In some places, skaters were used to long-distance skating down miles of frozen rivers.

One skater in 1876 noted that it was possible to cover twenty miles (32 km) in an hour. That's as fast as cars used to drive! The Acme skate, however, with its short blade, was not considered practical for this long-distance speed skating. Recognizing the need for a new kind of skate, James Whelpley invented the Long Reach skate.

Inventing the Long Reach Skate

Whelpley was only eighteen years old when he invented the Long Reach skate – named for a stretch of the St. John River near his home in New Brunswick. Whelpley thought "Long Reach" was a good name for a skate that was ideal for speeding down the frozen river.

As a young man, Whelpley was interested in mechanics and worked on grinding and

repairing skates in his spare time. He believed that if the blade of a skate was longer, it would be possible to skate faster. Whelpley tested his idea by making a skate with a blade that stretched beyond the front of the skater's boot, then asking a friend to try the experimental skates for him. He quickly discovered that the skate needed to be longer in both the front and the back to offer good balance. Sure enough, the longer blade worked. Soon many skaters in Long Reach were gliding up the river on Whelpley's seventeen-inch (43-cm) racing skate.

Together with his brothers, Joseph and Wilmot, James formed a company called the Whelpley Skate Factory. The factory opened in 1859, in Greenwich, New Brunswick, and manufactured skates that still used a wooden base. In 1868, Whelpley left his company and moved to Dartmouth to work at the Starr Manufacturing Company. While there, he invented a double grinder, which allowed a skate to be ground in one simple step rather than two.

Whelpley returned to Greenwich in 1875, after inventing a new kind of self-fastening skate that attached at the toe and the heel. He reopened the Whelpley Skate Factory with his brothers and twelve-year-old W. J. Cameron, who eventually became a talented machinist and foreman for the company. They advertised their product as "the simplest and most durable skate ever offered to the public." A pair of skates cost four dollars.

After spending a few years living and working in the United States, Whelpley returned once again to his hometown of Greenwich, New Brunswick, and bought back the Whelpley Skate Factory once again. The reopened J. A. Whelpley Factory continued to manufacture skates, producing twenty to twenty-five thousand pairs per year until the early 1890s, when Whelpley died.

Did you know that the first covered ice rinks were built around 1860? People realized that if the rink was protected by a roof, no one had to shovel the ice to clear it of snow. In the late 1800s, these rinks were often decorated extravagantly and bands were hired to play for fancy dress balls at which the skaters wore elaborate costumes.

Chapter 7

From Peach Baskets to Basketball

n the countryside near Almonte, Ontario, where the winters are long and snowy, James Naismith, the inventor of the game of basketball, was born on November 6, 1861. His father, John, was a builder. In 1869, John Naismith bought a sawmill in Fort Coulonge, Ontario, near Ottawa. He hoped that with his own sawmill, he would have a good supply of inexpensive lumber for his construction business. This would help him provide well for his young family. Unfortunately, things did not work out the way he wanted. In the summer of 1870, the sawmill burned down. James was just eight years old when his father's dreams for the sawmill were dashed.

In the fall of 1870, before the Naismiths had recovered from the loss of the sawmill, disease struck the family. There was an outbreak of typhoid, which brought with it fever, red spots, and abdominal pain. Today typhoid is easily treated with antibiotics, but in 1870 it could be deadly. When family members caught the illness, they were separated from the rest of the family to prevent everyone from getting ill.

James's father was the first to become sick. The children were taken away by their uncle while their mother stayed behind to nurse their father through his illness. Sadly, both parents died of typhoid later that fall. Eventually, James, together with his older sister and younger brother, went to live with his uncle Peter on a large farm in Almonte, Ontario.

Life in Almonte

The town of Almonte, with its large trees and flowing river, was an attractive place to grow up. It was a settlement of Scottish immigrants like James's own grandfather, who had worked hard to make a living in the same rugged rural area. James grew up going to the Presbyterian Church, and he developed a strong Christian faith, which would later influence his choice of career.

Living on the farm with his uncle Peter, James was expected to do his share of the chores. He once had an accident with a team of horses that was pulling a sleigh loaded with hay across an ice-covered river. The ice broke and the horses went through into the cold water, but James quickly sized up the situation and decided to unhitch the sleigh before it too went into the water. Then he scrambled to help the horses get a foothold and pull themselves onto the bank. When he looked up, he saw that his uncle had been watching him. Uncle Peter wanted James to learn how to solve problems and rely on himself for solutions, so he did not rush forward to help. From his uncle, James learned to be independent, hard-working, and confident of his own abilities.

Of course, life in Almonte was not all work. James and a group of boys would gather behind a nearby blacksmith shop to try to outdo each other with athletic stunts. Their contests were not restricted to swinging from limb to limb among the trees, however. They also tried to best each other lifting the anvil in the blacksmith's shop and playing tug-of-war with a long rope.

Did you know that young James's uncle would not buy his nephew ice skates? Undiscouraged, the resourceful boy took two old files and some strips of hickory wood and made himself a pair.

One of the games they played, called Duck on the Rock, later became important in the invention of basketball. Each of the boys would choose a "duck," which was a rock the size of a fist. One player was a guard and would place his duck on a large rock that sat behind the blacksmith's shop. The other boys would each take a turn trying to knock the duck off the rock. If a player missed the duck, he had to go get his rock before the guard could tag him. But if he knocked the duck down, the guard had to pick up the duck and put it back on the rock before trying to tag the boy who had just thrown. Whenever the guard managed to tag a player, they exchanged places.

The contests and games he played with the other boys, as well as the work he did on the farm, made James a strong and athletic young man. One friend remembered that even when James was working on the farm binding sheaves of wheat, a competition began. He would approach an unbound sheaf while still holding the one he had just bound. Tossing the bound one into the air, he would finish binding the next one before the first one touched the ground. Then he'd challenge anyone else to do the same thing. It was no wonder people admired Naismith's athletic ability.

University Days

Naismith decided to go to university and become a Presbyterian minister, so in 1883 he enrolled at McGill University in Montreal. At first, he focused only on his studies and did not get involved with any other activities. However, one day he was visited by two students who invited him to participate in the athletics program on campus. Naismith decided to visit the gym and see what was happening.

A man named Frederick Barnjum, who was interested in the study of physical fitness, was in charge of the Montreal Gymnastics Club, which he ran out of the gym at McGill. The gymnasium provided Barnjum with a place both to offer physical-education programs and to study the benefits of fitness. When Naismith first walked into the gym, he was impressed by the sight of students working at a number of different activities. Some were using equipment, such as parallel bars, barbells, bridge ladders, and the vaulting box, and others were performing tumbling routines. Naismith was attracted by both the physical challenge and the competitive spirit of Barnjum's program.

Did you know that Naismith felt that more than any money or fame, the sight of basketball hoops in out-of-the-way places gave him pleasure? He said that "deep in the Wisconsin woods an old barrel hoop nailed to a tree, or a weather-beaten shed on the Mexican border with a rusty iron hoop nailed to one end" reminded him that he had achieved his goal.

Naismith also played football at McGill. He got drawn into it while watching a football practice with a friend. When the center left the game with a broken nose, the captain called out to the spectators, "Won't one of you fellows come in and help us out?" Naismith looked around and, seeing no one come forward, took off his coat and joined the game. After that, he played regularly all through his years at college. This caused some consternation among his fellow students at the seminary, who frowned on football and athletics in general. Naismith was amused to learn that a group of his classmates had even gathered to pray for his soul.

An incident in a football game made Naismith reconsider his career choice. A teammate lost his temper during a difficult football game and cursed loudly. When he saw Naismith nearby, he quickly apologized, which surprised Naismith because he had never commented on his teammate's language. He came to the conclusion that his ability to play hard and still maintain self-control was an example to others, and that he could do good in athletics without going into the ministry.

Did you know that Naismith's sister, Anne, never forgave him for not going into the ministry? Naismith was eventually ordained in 1916 and served as a chaplain during the First World War.

After he graduated in 1890, Naismith enrolled at the YMCA training school in Springfield, Massachusetts. The YMCA, which offered religious and sports programs, allowed him to combine his interest in athletics with his commitment to the Christian faith.

Naismith Tests Some Ideas

At the YMCA training school the director, Luther Gulick, had a problem. During the winter months the instructors could find no indoor game that appealed to the students. The usual indoor activities included calisthenics, which developed strength in different groups of muscles. But after a while these exercises, which were repeated over and over, became boring. Gulick needed to find a more enjoyable activity. He organized a group of students and teachers to discuss the possibilities, but at first they made no progress.

In the meantime, the instructors took their students through various drills, marching exercises, and calisthenics. One teacher tried to combine gymnastics work with some

Muscular Christianity

In the nineteenth century, many Christians emphasized hard work and felt that recreational pastimes should be avoided. For this reason, Naismith's interest in athletics was frowned on by his uncle and his sister.

On the other hand, some members of the church began to view rigorous physical activity as a kind of Christianity applied to the body. Their beliefs were referred to as Muscular Christianity. This new way of thinking about athletics was what Naismith first encountered at the YMCA in the 1890s.

With the growth of cities during the Industrial Revolution, there was a concern for the moral health of people who lived in crowded urban areas. The YMCA's original programs were a response to this. By the 1850s, the YMCA had added sports and recreational activities as well. At first, this was very controversial, but eventually people came to accept it.

traditional track-and-field activities. None of these appealed very much to the students.

At this point, Naismith suggested that perhaps the problem was not with the students but with the type of activity they were trying. He thought they needed something that appealed to the students' sense of play. Gulick responded by putting Naismith in charge of the class.

Naismith thought that some type of game would be more popular than exercise routines, so he removed the apparatus from the gym and tried some contests that used different kinds of balls. Unfortunately, these games were not sophisticated enough to keep the students' interest for long.

Naismith knew that outdoor sports like football were popular with the men, and he thought perhaps it was possible to bring these outdoor games indoors. He wondered if it might work to play football using a tackle like that used in rugby. He thought this simple change might make the game less rough and more suitable for indoor play. But when he tried it, the students were not impressed. They liked football and did not want to play a "sissy" version of it.

Naismith then tried indoor soccer. Unfortunately, his students were not used to playing soccer in soft running shoes, and when they kicked the ball hard, they immediately regretted it. Naismith said that this class turned into a lesson on first aid instead of a soccer game. And there was another problem. When the students kicked the ball, windows were often broken and equipment knocked off the walls. Naismith needed a better idea.

A Whole New Game

Two weeks of classes had passed and Naismith had not yet found an answer to his problem. It seemed that the men were attached to the

Did you know that the dribble began as a defensive measure to allow a player to keep possession of the ball? For a brief period, players tried an overhead dribble, which involved batting the ball upward in the air.

sports they knew and did not like to see them changed. This meant devising a completely new game would be better than reworking an old one.

He tried to think what elements comprised the sports people liked, and he decided that they all used a ball. Games that used a small ball also used a bat or some other kind of stick. He had learned that his Canadian students knew how to handle a lacrosse stick but not a baseball bat, while the Americans were comfortable with the bat but not with the lacrosse stick. In order to make the game easy for anyone to learn, Naismith decided to use a large, light ball and no stick or bat.

Next, Naismith thought about how popular American football was. Unfortunately, the rough tackle used in football would be a problem in an indoor game. He realized that the reason for the tackle was that a player who had the ball was allowed to run with it. Once a player was running, the tackle was the only way to stop him. Naismith sat up in his chair. He realized that if a player could not run with the ball, there was no reason for a tackle. Here were the first principles of his new game!

Refining the Details

The next question was what kind of goal would work. Naismith first considered the goal used in lacrosse, which was simply a space six feet (1.8 m) high and eight feet (2.4 m) wide between two posts. In lacrosse, the harder the ball is thrown, the more likely it is that a goal will be scored. But Naismith did not want the ball to be thrown hard in an indoor game because he thought this would lead to injuries.

He found himself remembering his childhood game of Duck on a Rock. In that game, a gentle toss of the player's rock in an arc was strategically better than a hard throw. A hard throw would mean that the player had farther to run to get his rock back, and that left more chance of being tagged. A gently tossed rock would still knock down the duck, but would also make the player's rock easier to retrieve before the guard could tag him out.

Having decided that he wanted his new game to make use of this kind of gently arcing throw, Naismith then imagined that the goal could be something like a box on the floor.

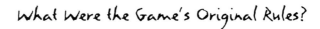

What Were the Game's Original Rules?

The set of thirteen rules that James Naismith pinned to the bulletin board in 1891 was first published in the school newspaper in January 1892. They read as follows:

1. The ball may be thrown in any direction with one or both hands.
2. The ball may be batted in any direction with one or both hands (never with the fist).
3. A player cannot run with the ball. The player must throw it from the spot on which he catches it; allowance to be made for a man who catches the ball when running at a good speed.
4. The ball must be held in or between the hands; the arms or body must not be used for holding it.
5. No shouldering, holding, pushing, tripping or striking in any way the person of an opponent shall be allowed; the first infringement of this rule by any person shall count as a foul, the second shall disqualify him until the next goal is made, or, if there was evident intent to injure the person, for the whole of the game, no substitute allowed.
6. A foul is striking the ball with the fist, violation of Rules 3, 4, and such as described in Rule 5.
7. If either side makes three consecutive fouls, it shall count a goal for the opponents. (Consecutive means without the opponents in the meantime making a foul.)
8. A goal shall be made when the ball is thrown or batted from the grounds into the basket and stays there, providing those defending the goal do not touch or disturb the goal. If the ball rests on the edge and the opponent moves the basket, it shall count as a goal.
9. When the ball goes out of bounds, it shall be thrown into the field and played by the person first touching it. In case of a dispute, the umpire shall throw it straight into the field. The thrower-in is allowed five seconds. If he holds it longer it shall go to the opponent. If any side persists in delaying the game, the umpire shall call a foul on them.
10. The umpire shall be judge of the men and shall note the fouls and notify the referee when three consecutive fouls have been made. He shall have the power to disqualify men according to Rule 5.
11. The referee shall be judge of the ball and shall decide when the ball is in play, in bounds, to which side it belongs, and shall keep the time. He shall decide when a goal has been made, and keep account of the goals, with any other duties that are usually performed by a referee.
12. The time shall be two fifteen-minute halves with five minutes' rest between.
13. The side making the most goals in that time shall be declared winners. In case of a draw, the game may, by agreement of the captains, be continued until another goal is made.

But there was a problem with this idea. When the defense protected the goal, it would be almost impossible to score. Obviously the goal needed to be higher, preferably above the players' heads. Finally, Naismith determined that he would start the game by tossing the ball up between one player from each side. Now he was ready to try it out.

The Very First Game

First, there was some equipment needed. Naismith looked at the balls that were available in his office and decided to use the soccer ball. Then he asked the custodian for two boxes, but he only had two peach baskets. Naismith nailed the baskets to the lower railing of the balcony, with one at either end of the gym. He then had the secretary type out his rules, which he posted on the notice board.

Naismith was standing with the soccer ball in his hands and the two baskets nailed to the balcony when the first student arrived and said, "Huh! Another new game?" Right away, Naismith worried that the game might be doomed. When the rest of the class arrived, he promised that this would be the last experiment he would try on them.

From the beginning, the game was a success. At first there were many fouls and the players did not know how to play together

A Game for Women, Too

Within a month of the game's invention, women were playing basketball. One day, teachers from the nearby Buckingham Grade School overheard the cheers from the YMCA gym. Intrigued, they walked in and were soon caught up in the excitement of the game. When they asked Naismith if women could play too, he agreed to set up a time for them to have the gym.

They first played the game in their street clothes, which were long dresses with mutton-shaped sleeves. Soon two teams were formed, and when a tournament was suggested in March 1892, even the wives of the YMCA faculty were asked to play. One participant was a young woman called Maude Sherman, who later married James Naismith.

In 1893, a game was played between two teams of women at Smith College. The newspaper reported that the hall was beautifully decorated with green bunting and lavender flags, and that no men were allowed to watch because the women wore bloomers to play.

All-Black Teams Show Fans How the Game Is Played

By the 1920s, the most famous basketball team was the original Celtics of New York. The only team that was a match for the Celtics was an all-black team, the New York Renaissance, called the Rens. Even though the press rarely reported on the achievements of the Rens, the fans knew that their excellent teamwork and superior passing skills were the reason that, by 1932, they had won 473 games and lost only 49 over four seasons.

The Rens never called a time-out, preferring instead to demonstrate their stamina to the opposing team (who, at the point of exhaustion, would be forced to ask for time-out themselves). When the Rens played, the ball seldom touched the ground. They were known for a fast-passing game with almost no dribbling.

Because of racism, black players had tremendous challenges to overcome. When they were on the road, they could not stay in hotels and would not be served in most restaurants. Sometimes the Rens had to sleep in their custom-made bus, but more often they would drive as much as 200 miles (320 km) to and from games to return to their headquarters in the major cities.

as a team, but this quickly improved. Word got out that Naismith's class was fun, and soon there was an audience for the games. During the Christmas vacation, some students introduced the game at their local YMCAs. When one student, Frank Mahan, returned from vacation, he asked Naismith what he would call the game, suggesting that it could be called Naismith Ball. When Naismith laughed, saying that name might kill the game, Frank said, "Why not call it basketball?"

Chapter 8

A New Spin on Bowling

Bowling, sometimes called **kegling**, has been traced back as far as 5200 B.C. in Egypt, though little is known about the Egyptian game. It was later played in third-century Germany, where it was a religious rite in which the pins represented people without moral principles. The devout would roll a ball down the length of a church cloister, hoping to knock down a pin, or kegel, at the other end. If a person failed to knock down a pin, that meant his spiritual life needed some work. In the Middle Ages, Protestant reformer Martin Luther even built a bowling alley for his children and enjoyed watching them play. He used the example of being humbled by playing poorly to illustrate the importance of avoiding boastful pride.

Modern Bowling Is Born

From this early history, bowling evolved into a sport that, in England and North America, was frowned on by the church. It was associated with gambling, drinking, and other disreputable pastimes such as billiards and card-playing.

In the early 1900s, a Toronto entrepreneur named Thomas F. Ryan tried to clean up this image of bowling by opening the Temperance Street Bowling Club. He decorated his club in a luxurious southern plantation style, with potted palms, ceiling fans, and a piano. Ryan was even known to provide a string orchestra for his members, who were the elite of Toronto society.

When it opened in 1905, the Temperance Street Bowling Club provided the ten-pin game, which had become the common version in the United States and Canada. At first, the new club was a success, but Tommy Ryan gradually realized that he would need to adapt to his members' needs if he wanted to stay in business.

Many of the club's bowlers were businessmen who liked to play during their lunch hour but found the game took too long to finish. One day, to speed up the game, the men instructed the **pinboys** to set up five pins rather than ten. Ryan immediately saw the possibilities. Besides being quicker to finish, a five-pin game was easier on Ryan's high-class clientele, who found that the ball used in the ten-pin game was too heavy to throw. Ryan understood his members well, and joked that "some hadn't used their muscles in years. They'd bowl one or two games, then play bridge in my office while I supplied adhesive tape for their thumbs."

How Was the New Game Different?

Tommy Ryan began to work out his new version of bowling. He had his father take

Duckpin and Candlepin Bowling

Prior to inventing his new game, Tommy Ryan had tried both duckpin and candlepin bowling with his members. These games used lighter balls and smaller pins. Ryan's members were dissatisfied with these versions, however, because it was difficult to knock down all ten pins with only two balls. Ryan explained that this was the reason he added a third ball to his five-pin game. Finally, he replaced the large sixteen-pound (7-kg) ball with the smaller three-and-a-half-pound (1.5-kg) ball used in duckpins and candlepins.

Did you know that the first pins used in the five-pin game were so light that, when hit, they sometimes flew right through the window of the bowling club and landed on the street below?

some old bowling pins and carve them down to a smaller size on a woodworker's lathe. He then arranged five of these modified pins on the triangle used in the ten-pin game. The new scoring system numbered the pins from left to right, 4-2-1-3-5, and required that the counter pin, number four, be knocked over before a player could score any points.

Inevitably, there were some early problems with the new invention. The smaller, lighter pins allowed the ball to pass right between them and had a tendency to fly about with a great racket when they were hit. The pinboys, who had the job of setting up the pins, had to be careful to stay well away once the game began or risk being battered by flying pins. Ryan solved these problems by making the pins slightly larger and attaching a band of rubber around the widest part. These

A Sport for Families

Ryan's 1909 invention brought many important changes. Not only was the five-pin game quicker, but the smaller ball made the game more appealing for women, a group Ryan considered key to the future growth of bowling. Marion Dibble, who in 1921 formed the first ladies' league with Mabel McDowell, remembers: "It wasn't considered nice for ladies to go into bowling houses in those days, so I used to slip down early in the mornings and bowl and be gone before the men arrived for lunch."

With the growth of the ladies' leagues, more and more women took up bowling, and soon it was even being thought of as a sport suitable for families. This was a significant change from its earlier associations with drinking and gambling.

two innovations made the pins easier to hit and reduced both the noise and the problem of pins crashing around.

There were numerous changes to the five-pin game over the years, including the invention in the 1930s of leather bowling shoes to cut down on the damage to the floors, the introduction of automatic pinsetters in 1957, the elimination of the counter pin, and the development of a new scoring system that counted the pins as 2-3-5-3-2.

Tommy Ryan never patented his invention, and as a result missed out on a fortune as the game spread. With all the other business ventures he was operating, he just forgot. When asked about it later, he said, "I don't really care about the millions of dollars I could have made as long as people are having fun."

Chapter 9

Taming Winter with the Snowmobile

The strange-looking contraption roared through the streets of Valcourt, Quebec, on January 31, 1922. People yelled and dashed up out of the way, all the while staring at this fascinating machine that had dogs barking, cats fleeing for safety, and horses bucking. That young Bombardier boy had come up with another invention, and this one traveled over snowy streets on runners instead of wheels. The citizens of Valcourt were watching the test run of the first snowmobile. They were also watching a very angry Monsieur Bombardier running after his two sons, shouting and waving his arms at them. Some Valcourt citizens still remember the sight of Léopold pulling on ropes to steer, while Armand sat behind his younger brother, having jumped on after starting the vehicle. They say that the boys drove the machine for more than a mile, until Léopold could not hold the ropes any more and it crashed into a barn.

58

For weeks over their Christmas holidays, Armand and Léopold had worked in secret in their garage, building Armand's latest invention. Armand's father had become so frustrated with his son's constant tinkering with the family car that he bought him a broken Model-T Ford. Armand took the engine out of the car and repaired it, attaching it to the back of an old sleigh. Then he carved a wooden propeller and put it on the back of the engine by fixing it to the radiator fan shaft. Ropes were tied to the two front runners of the sleigh so the driver could steer. Armand built his own parts when he could not find ones he needed, like the propeller. But he could not find a muffler to fit, and did not try to build one, so there was nothing to stifle the loud noise of the engine. Although fifteen-year-old Armand was thrilled with the success of his new invention, his father furiously ordered him to dismantle it. Still, the snowmobile was just the latest in Armand's long line of inventions, and it was to flavor his pursuits for the rest of his life.

An Inventive Boyhood

Armand had always been fascinated by the way things worked. In fact, he showed such a mechanical gift that his father let Armand use his tools and woodworking shop for his experiments. Armand used spare parts and small pieces of machinery to build toys for his seven younger brothers and sisters. He even worked on repairing engines. The men laughed at the young boy when he first told them that he could fix engines that would not start in the winter, but they stopped laughing when he proved himself repeatedly.

Armand worked making deliveries for his parents' general store and helping the priest with Sunday Mass. He used his earnings to buy tiny clock and watch parts from the local jeweler. In fact, all his money went toward his experiments with machines. He designed and built toy tractors, trains, and even a paddle boat with a motor. All of the toys worked. The boat paddled on the river, creating quite a stir among the local children.

Unfortunately, Armand was more concerned with making his designs work than he was conscious about safety. When he was fifteen, he decided to build a steam engine and convinced his aunt to give him some used sewing-machine parts. With a friend's help, he soldered the pieces together with other parts he'd found, like tubes, valves, a boiler, a piston, and a tire pump. He convinced his aunt to let him attach the contraption to her sewing machine to try it out, but when he used a car tire to send air pressure in, the engine worked the sewing machine so fast that his aunt was scared her nephew would break it. Armand and his friend, however, were so excited that they ran and told some of the townspeople about the invention. Several men were working on the church's broken heating system and allowed Armand to bring his steam engine in the next day to

see if it would work with real steam. Sure enough, it did – for a few seconds. Then it blew up.

A couple of Armand's other inventions also ended with a bang. When the boy was fourteen, the town veterinarian gave him a broken pistol. In one week, Armand repaired the firing mechanism, shortened the barrel, and built and attached two small wooden wheels. Proudly he went over to show the veterinarian what he had done. Although the doctor was concerned, he was also impressed with Armand and wanted to support his inventiveness. So he put a little gunpowder in the miniature cannon to try it out. The result: a loud *bang!* The cannon worked. The veterinarian told Armand that he must never use the cannon again, and that he must not tell anyone what he had made. But Valcourt was a small town. Neighbors came to see what had made the bang and word soon spread about the Bombardier boy's latest experiment.

Garage Bombardier

Armand's parents wanted him to become a priest, but Armand wished to be a mechanic. He wanted to study engineering, electricity, and mechanics, not Greek, Latin, and theology. Armand pestered his parents until, finally, they agreed to let him become a mechanic's apprentice. He apprenticed during the day, and spent his nights studying electrical engineering and mechanics, and reading every journal he could find on science and technology – especially ones that described new advances and discoveries. By the time Armand was seventeen, he was a first-class mechanic working in Montreal.

> Did you know that the family business that Bombardier set up has become a multinational corporation with offices in countries all over the world? Since Armand's death, Bombardier Inc. has built aircraft, trains, subway cars, invented the Sea-Doo, and made parts for NASA's lunar modules.

But Armand missed his hometown and his family missed him, so his father bought land and built a garage to give Armand his own business back home. In May 1926, at just nineteen, Armand opened Garage Bombardier.

He already had a reputation in Valcourt because of all the things he did growing up, and he was such a great mechanic that his reputation just got better and his business boomed. Soon it was so successful that he had to expand and hire employees. Meanwhile, Armand kept studying by correspondence. He taught himself English so he could read and learn more about machines, and he studied accounting so he could manage his business efficiently. And Armand was still inventive. When he could not find the equipment to make what he wanted, he designed it himself, then manufactured the parts. When Armand wanted to have electricity in his garage, for example, he generated his own power by damming up the river and building his own mini hydro-electric plant. Garage Bombardier had electricity long before the village of Valcourt did.

The Birth of the Snow Car

By the 1920s, cars were driven by many people, not just the wealthy. But there were no snowplows to clear the roads in the winter, so the only ways to get around were by snowshoe, ski, dogsled, or horse and sleigh. With no cars on the roads, there was no repair work for Bombardier's garage. Needing something to do with his spare time, Bombardier devoted his winters to designing a vehicle that would travel easily through the snow. When he saw the grooves left by the runners on the horse-drawn sleighs, he had an idea. What if he could make a car that ran in the grooves left

by the sleighs? He got a car and moved the front wheels so that they were as close together as the sleigh grooves in the snow, then tried it out. The car worked, but the back wheels spun. So Bombardier added an extra set of wheels on the back and wrapped chains around them for better traction in the snow. Now the machine could move, but it still was not what he wanted.

Did you know that before the Ski-Doo was invented, people in Labrador tried making snowshoes for their horses so they could travel through deep snow in winter?

Next, Bombardier put runners, or skis, on the front instead of wheels, narrowed the double sets of back wheels and put them closer together, and put a steel track around them instead of chains. He drove around in the new "snow car" (*auto-neige*) and it worked. Charles Boisvert, the owner of the local hotel, bought the first one and used it to drive customers between the hotel and the train station, just over a mile (2 km) away. Bombardier sold twelve more of these snow cars between 1928 and 1930. Finally, people had a way to travel the roads in the winter.

Eventually, Bombardier noticed that his steel track dented the wheels of his snow cars over time. So he made a rubber track and

used old brake drums for wheels. By 1931, he had a snow car that had six smaller wheels covered with a rubber track. An order of Benedictine monks from the nearby Saint-Benoit-du-Lac monastery heard about Bombardier's invention and came to the workshop asking to see the snow vehicle for themselves. Bombardier took them for a test drive and they bought the snow car right then. Later, these monks had the first snow-mobile accident! One day, they decided to take a short cut across a lake, but the ice was not thick enough to carry a vehicle full of people. The ice cracked under them and their snow vehicle began to sink. Luckily, the monks all had time to get out, and some men brought a **winch** and rescued the snow car before it sank completely.

By 1933, Bombardier had designed a two-person snow car with skis in front and back. He built his own motor and put it in upside down, at the rear of the car. Like his first effort, the one he and Léopold had built when they were boys, this snow car had no reverse gear and was driven by a propeller at the back. The body looked like a plane's cockpit with its sleek design. Bombardier had designed it out of plywood and canvas, and he hired the village carriage maker to build it. Again, he had a snow machine that traveled but was not perfect.

With all of the work that he had done on snow cars, he now knew that there were three keys to a successful vehicle: the weight had to be evenly distributed throughout the vehicle so the car did not tip or sink on one side while traveling; the **propulsion** system (the engine) had to be safe, reliable, and able to be cooled while running; and the **suspension** needed to be good enough to give passengers a comfortable ride. Bombardier wanted to produce a small vehicle that one or two people could ride, but he could not find an engine compact enough and well-cooled enough to suit a small vehicle. And for once, Bombardier could not design one – the technology did not exist yet.

A Personal Mission

Bombardier continued to spend every winter working on his snow cars. One night, while he was working in his garage, he received an urgent message to get home. When he arrived, he found that his two-year-old son, Yvon, was critically ill with appendicitis. The doctor said that Yvon would have to be taken to the hospital in Sherbrooke, thirty miles (50 km) away, if he was going to survive. Bombardier had a garage full of snow-car parts, but he did not have one snow car put together. Sadly, there was no way for him to get Yvon to the hospital through the snow-blocked roads, and Yvon died that night. Bombardier and his wife, Yvonne, were devastated, and Bombardier decided that he would work even harder to create a snow vehicle so no one else would have to suffer because of blocked roads in winter.

With his increased determination, Bombardier created a new, larger snow car. He still used skis on the front, but now he had two rubber-covered tracks on the back. Each track ran over a line of three wheels. At the front was a rubber-covered wooden sprocket wheel with twelve cogs (like teeth), which Bombardier designed. As the sprocket wheel turned, the cogs fit into spaces along the track and sent it back around two bigger wheels. The track remained in contact with the ground even between the two wheels, not just where each wheel touched the road. Together, the sprocket wheel and the track

absorbed any shocks. Bombardier also kept the engine in the rear. He found that the snow car got better traction (and propulsion) this way, so it did not slip as much, was easier to turn, and went faster. This new snow car still looked like a car, but the treads from the new track were like a tank's and they kept the car on top of the snow. Bombardier wanted his machine to be able to travel anywhere, not just on the roads.

By this point, Bombardier was working on snow vehicles all year long. Finally pleased with his new snow car, he decided to publicize it and sell it. Instead of spending money on advertising, however, Bombardier traveled around Quebec showing off his *auto-neige*. He would travel to a town and take the local newspaper reporter for a ride in his new vehicle. After each test drive, the journalists wrote about Bombardier and his new snow car for their local papers. Soon, everyone wanted to find out more about this new car that traveled over the snow.

When Bombardier got home from his publicity tour, he improved his sprocket wheel and track system and his snow car and applied for **patents** for them. Now his car had two large wheels with a small wheel between them on each side of the back, a parallel bar holding all three wheels together, rubber belts and crosslinks, and rubber-covered cast-iron and nickel sprockets. This was a far cry from just putting chains around the wheels at the back. On June 29, 1937, Bombardier received his patents, which gave him seventeen years to be the only one to make his snow cars and track system. If any one else made them, they needed to have Bombardier's permission.

The Success of the B7

Bombardier called his first patented snow car, the B7, his "original heavy work-horse" because it could replace a horse-team. It was called the B7 because it could fit seven passengers. The B was for Bombardier. Bombardier made and sold fifty B7s, mainly to police, doctors, funeral directors, milkmen, traveling salespeople, missionaries, telephone companies, school boards, and mail-delivery people. Bombardier even trained and hired mechanics to build and look after his B7s. No longer did townspeople watch Bombardier taking off to test drive his new snow car and walking back when it broke down.

With the success of the B7, Bombardier changed the name of his business from Garage Bombardier to L'Auto-Neige Bombardier (Bombardier Snowmobile) in the spring of 1937. Even though his father and others warned him that he had built up a good business as a mechanic, and that this

Working for the Allies

During the Second World War, like many other businessmen and inventors, Bombardier was asked to work for the war effort. The government of Canada knew about Bombardier's success with snow cars, so it asked him to design a winter troop carrier to take soldiers into the battlefields and remote locales of northern Europe.

Bombardier modified his B12 and changed his patented track system to create an all-terrain vehicle for the army. The Canadian Forces called this troop carrier the B1. It had two skis on the front, four large wheels on each side, wide tracks, doors on both sides, a hatch in the roof, hydraulic brakes, and places to put guns. Bombardier also created other military machines, but his most famous was the Penguin, which he designed in 1943.

The Penguin was low to the ground, carried only two people, had eight wheels on each side, and tracks a yard (almost 1 m) wide that ran the whole length of the vehicle. The tracks angled upward in front of the first wheels. The Penguin started easily, even in temperatures of forty degrees below zero, was an all-terrain vehicle, and even floated if you strapped barrels on it.

might not be a safe business move, especially since he and his wife had five children at home, Bombardier was determined. He wanted to devote all of his time to developing his snowmobiles. He kept producing B7s and also made a B12, which fit twelve passengers.

After the war, towns and cities began to plow the snow off the roads in winter to make it easier for cars to travel all year round. Bombardier knew that he needed to develop some new machines because his snow cars would not be in such great demand. He decided to travel across Canada to see what the land was like in other parts of the country and how he could adapt his inventions to suit other needs. He saw how hard it was for people in the lumber camps of northern Quebec and Ontario to load and move the logs from the forest to the lumber mill. Five or six men worked for hours with a horse-drawn sled. So in 1949, Bombardier made the BT, a machine with a winch and a loading platform for logs. One person using the BT replaced six men and their workhorses. In the Alberta oil fields, Bombardier saw **muskeg** for the first time. Muskeg is the Native name for swampy land. Sometimes workers looking for oil would sink into the muskeg up to their waists, and equipment would disappear entirely. To deal with this, Bombardier invented the TN, a truck-snowmobile, in 1950. It had the engine in the front, interchangeable front wheels and skis, and a large drilling platform on the back. Bombardier also invented the TD Truck,

The Muskeg Tractor

In 1953, Bombardier introduced the Muskeg Tractor, an all-terrain vehicle that moved easily through the mud and swamp. The "Muskeg" was in such demand that Bombardier sold it all over the world: Japan, Africa, Alaska, Australia, and even to workers moving sand in the Sahara Desert. In 1957, Sir Vivian Fuchs and his team used Muskeg Tractors to travel to the South Pole in Antarctica.

After the tractor, Bombardier invented the Muskeg Carrier. It was bigger than the Muskeg Tractor and could carry up to four tons of cargo. This machine was especially used by the forest industry because it could load 6,500 pounds (3,000 kg) of wood in seven seconds. Muskeg Carriers were also used to lay the Trans-Canada Pipeline in the 1950s.

which had wide tracks in the front and back to give good traction and support.

Inventing the Ski-Dog

Bombardier always had it in mind to make a snow car that could carry one or two passengers, travel quickly over any type of snow, and go into almost any area. One of his biggest obstacles, however, had been finding a small, air-cooled engine. During the Second

Did you know that in 1968, Ralph Plaisted, from Minneapolis, arranged for himself and some friends to travel to the North Pole by Ski-Doo? It took them forty-three days to get there. On the return trip, the weather was so mild that the ice and snow started melting. The adventurers had to be rescued by ski-plane. Since the plane could fit only three Ski-Doos on board, one is still out on the tundra somewhere!

World War, much progress had been made in engine design, and by the 1950s small engines were available. At last, he had the three elements he wanted in a snow vehicle: a small engine, skis on the front, and a single track in the rear. It would be like a motorcycle for snow.

Bombardier had always been frustrated that his large snow vehicles often carried only one person, which seemed like such a waste to him. With this new small machine, that problem was solved. After experimenting with different bodies and engines, he settled on a four-cycle motor, a wooden frame fitting one to two people, wooden skis in front, a fifteen-inch (39-cm) track in the back, and handlebars for steering. Bombardier called his new vehicle the Ski-Dog because he hoped it would replace the dogsled.

Once he had built one, Bombardier set off to test it. He wanted to try it in the Arctic, where he thought it would be used the most, so he headed for James Bay. He traveled by car, then train, then airplane with his Ski-Dog, over the five hundred miles (800 km) north in early 1952. He knew that there would be a lot of snow there, and he could test his invention for days.

When he arrived, his friend Maurice Ouimet met him. Bombardier and Ouimet had grown up together in Valcourt, and now his friend was an Oblate mission priest in the Arctic. Father Ouimet was happy to see his old friend, and even happier to be involved in testing Bombardier's newest invention. When Bombardier was ready, he started up his Ski-Dog and roared off across the snow. More and more people gathered to watch the strange machine, and Bombardier let them take turns trying it out. They loved it! For days, they test drove it and offered Bombardier comments and suggestions.

In the spring of 1952, Bombardier returned to Valcourt. He took into account all of the comments the people had made and refined his Ski-Dog. He changed the wooden skis to metal ones, put in springs to make the ride more comfortable, used a better two-cycle engine, and added headlights in case people had to drive the Ski-Dog at night. By 1959, his new machine was ready for sale to the public.

When the printer was making up the advertisements for the Ski-Dog, he misprinted the name as Ski-Doo. Fortunately, Bombardier liked the sound of that and decided to keep it. In that first year, he sold 225 Ski-Doos. Many people whom Bombardier had never thought

of as Ski-Doo customers bought them, like police officers and farmers, but his biggest surprise came when people started buying his machine for pleasure. After the Second World War, people had more money to spend on all things, including recreation. Unlike the B7, Bombardier's small Ski-Doo was affordable for many people. It was fun and fast and easy to handle, and it could go places that cars could not. The driver controlled the speed by squeezing the throttle on the handle, and there were no gears. It was easy to steer and anyone could learn to operate it in a few minutes. People quickly took to roaring over the countryside and racing each other.

Bombardier was very pleased. He had invented not only a method of transportation, but also a sport! In fact, Bombardier enjoyed

snowmobiling himself. He always had a reputation as a fast driver – now he did it over snow.

Today the snowmobile is still used for both transportation and recreation. Police, trappers, clergy, and doctors, among others, continue to use it to travel in northern climates and through woods in the winter. Ranchers use it to look after their cattle in the winter, and in Lapland, farmers use snowmobiles to herd reindeer. Meanwhile, the popularity of the sport of snowmobiling just keeps growing. There are now thousands of miles of groomed trails and more than ten thousand snowmobile clubs in North America alone.

Chapter 10

Racing Ahead in the Laser Sailboat

When people hear the word *laser*, most think of light beams, but a sailor pictures a small, sleek, one-person sailboat racing through the waves. Since it first came on the market in 1971, the Laser sailboat has revolutionized sailing worldwide. That's not bad for something that began as a sketch made during a telephone call!

The Million-Dollar Doodle

In 1969, the industrial designer and Olympic sailor Ian Bruce was designing a line of camping equipment for a Canadian outdoors company. As an added feature, the company asked Bruce to build a small boat that could be carried on a cartop for a camping trip. Since Bruce had never designed a boat, he decided to consult with someone who had. He telephoned his friend Bruce Kirby, a boat designer and Olympic sailor who worked in Chicago. During the conversation, Bruce explained the concept of this new boat.

The company had three main requirements. First, it had to be easy to build, so it could be sold at an affordable price; second, it had to be sporty and attractive, so it would appeal to sailors; and third, it needed to be lightweight, so almost anyone could pop it on the car and take it along. As Bruce and Kirby discussed the idea, Kirby sketched. By the end of the call, he had a basic design for the boat. Since then, Bruce Kirby has earned more than a million dollars in royalties for designing the Laser, and this first drawing has been nicknamed "the million-dollar doodle."

What Is Displacement?

A Greek mathematician, Archimedes, discovered that when a body is put in water, it displaces, or changes the position of, an amount of water equal to the body's own weight. This is called Archimedes' Principle of Buoyancy. You can see this principle at work when you get in the bathtub and the water level changes. Although it looks as though there's more water in the tub, this is really just the water that is being moved by the weight of your body. In fact, this is how Archimedes first found out about displacement. He noticed that the more of himself he put in a bath, the higher the water level rose.

He was so excited about his discovery that he jumped out of the bath and ran naked through the street yelling, "Eureka! Eureka!" which means "I've found it! I've found it!"

A boat displaces water the same way, but lakes and oceans are so large that we cannot see any change in the water level. The buoyancy of a boat is its ability to float in water.

Bruce Kirby knew, however, that the company requesting the boat might not ever build it. Often a firm has an idea for a product but does not follow through on it. The company might decide that it's too expensive, or that not enough people would buy it, or just to concentrate on other kinds of products. But Kirby liked the idea of a small sailboat, and he believed that even if the original company decided not to produce it, another firm might want a "high-performance dinghy."

Having come up with the basic design, Kirby next considered the technical aspects of building a boat, including the calculations for most effective sail size and area, the ideal weight of the crew, and the best displacement-length ratio (the weight of the boat in relation to its length). He wanted the boat to be lightweight, so it would be easy to manage and would not require a large, strong person to lift it or control it on the water. But it also had to be durable.

For extra strength in the **hull**, the part of the boat that sits in the water, Kirby fit foam strips on each side of the centerline. He also figured out that for good performance, the hull's waterline needed to be a minimum of twelve and a half feet (3.8 m) long, so he worked with that length. He also designed a foam-cored deck to fit over the hull. Kirby and Bruce named this hull-deck joint a "rollover **join**," and this is what gives the Laser its distinctive look. It also makes the boat strong.

A small, light hull needs a large sail. Kirby decided that seventy-six square feet (7 m²) was the ideal area for the sail. Because the little boat was meant to be transported and sailed easily, he wanted to make attaching the sail fast and simple. Usually, sails attach to masts with ropes and pulleys, or the sail gets pulled up the mast through a track. On his little boat, Kirby decided to have the sail pull over the mast just like a very long sock.

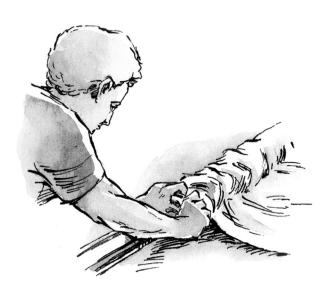

Racing for America's Teacup

By mid-October 1969, Bruce Kirby had finished the plans for the boat's basic design. He sent his drawings to Ian Bruce in Montreal. But the company that hired Bruce to build the boat had decided that it did not want it after all, so Bruce tucked the drawings into an office drawer. Then, in early 1970, the magazine that Bruce Kirby edited, *One Design*

and Offshore Yachtsman, decided to hold a regatta for small boats costing less than a thousand dollars. Playing on the name of the famous America's Cup race, the organizers called it the America's Teacup. It was planned for October 1970. Kirby thought of the little sailboat that he had designed for Ian Bruce, and he suggested that their boat would be perfect to make and try out at the Teacup. Ian Bruce agreed, and began building it.

The two men needed someone to design and build the sail, so they asked Hans Fogh, another Olympic sailor and a sailmaker in Toronto. Kirby, Bruce, and Fogh worked for months. Kirby was in Chicago, Illinois; Bruce in Dorval, Quebec; and Fogh in Toronto, Ontario. There were no fax machines then, so the three communicated by telephone and mail. In fact, Fogh built the sail without ever actually seeing the mast it would fit on. When they were almost done, they realized their little boat needed a name, so Kirby and Bruce decided to call it the Weekender. Fogh stitched TGIF, for Thank God It's Friday, on the sail.

The day before the race, Ian Bruce packed up the boat he had built, with the glue still drying on it, and set off from Dorval. First, he drove to Toronto, where he picked up Hans Fogh and the sail. Then they drove to Lake Geneva, Wisconsin, for the regatta, arriving early the next morning. That day, the three men came together for the first time. Excitedly, they assembled the **prototype** on the beach just before the first race. Fogh, who had won a silver medal in sailing at the 1960 Olympics, sailed their Weekender. He tied for first, a good showing for the new boat. But Fogh knew that he could improve it. While he was sailing, he felt the amount of bend in the mast and noticed that the curve of the sail did not work as well with the mast bend as it could. That evening, he took off the sail and recut it. When he sailed the next day, Fogh noticed that the new cut improved the boat immediately – so much so that he won the race!

What Are the Parts of a Sailboat?

Simply put, the hull and the **rig** together compose a sailboat. The hull is the boat's body. Its deck is the cover that you stand on, and that is what keeps water out of the hull. The underbody is the part of the hull that is under the water. A centerboard juts down into the water in the middle of the underbody and this is what keeps the boat from being blown over sideways or drifting off course. At the back of the underbody is the **rudder**, which steers the boat. The front of the boat, called the bow, is thinner than the back, or stern. This allows the hull to cut into the water and send it back against the curved underbody. As the water flows toward the stern, it squeezes against the boat and pushes it forward.

The top part of the sailboat is called the rig. It consists of the sail, mast, boom, and rigging. The **mast** is the long pole that runs up from the boat toward the sky. It attaches to a socket in the hull called the **mast step**. The boom is another, shorter pole that attaches horizontally to the mast and can pivot around it. The **luff**, or long forward edge of the sail, fits along the mast, while the **foot**, or lower edge of the sail, fits along the boom. Sailors use ropes called running rigging, which attach to the sail, to maneuver the boom and the sail. The standing rigging supports the mast, which "stands up."

It is the rig that captures the wind and produces motion. The hull's **waterline** is the place where the boat makes contact with the water. The waterline's length is measured from the bow to the stern. The longer a boat is along its waterline, the faster it will travel, so small boats need larger sail areas than large boats to travel rapidly. But the sail must not be too big, or the wind will just blow the boat over. The shape and area of the sail, the flexibility of the mast, and the shape of the hull must all be designed to work together to send the sailboat easily and quickly through the water. The weight of the crew is important, too. The heavier a boat is, the farther it sinks into the water. So too much or too little weight in the hull means that the boat displaces a different amount of water than intended. This puts the waterline at a different level, making it a different length than it's meant to be and therefore making the boat more difficult to sail.

The little Weekender, with its light purple hull, pink deck, and good performance, generated a lot of interest and excitement in sailing circles – especially among the three men who made it! After the regatta, Kirby, Bruce, and Fogh examined the boat and discussed ways to improve it. With the success of the first prototype, they knew that they had a good boat. The winds at the Teacup had been light, however, and the men knew that they needed to test the boat in a variety of wind speeds. They wanted their boat to perform just as well in strong winds as it did in light breezes.

The First Laser

The men took their observations from the Teacup race and set out to make a second prototype. Kirby moved the mast three inches (7.5 cm) forward, and tested different materials for it. The mast had been too flexible, so he used stiffer material on the bottom and also made it a foot (30 cm) longer. This let the sailor get the greatest maximum bend

Did you know that wind blowing into a sail produces energy? The mast and boom transmit this energy to the boat's hull, and this moves the boat forward through the water.

out of the mast, but still have good control. He made the sail's luff, which runs vertically, three inches (7.5 cm) longer, and the foot, which runs horizontally, two inches (5 cm) shorter. The sail changed shape, but the area always stayed at seventy-six square feet (7 m²). Then Kirby did a third sailplan, which allowed for a greater range of weights of crew to be able to sail the boat. Bruce added a mast step that moved fore (forward) and aft (backward), to help adjust the boat's balance in varying winds. Fogh tested new materials for the sail.

A month later, they were ready to launch again. In late November 1970, Kirby came up from Connecticut, where he now lived, and met Bruce and Fogh at the Royal St. Lawrence Yacht Club, near Montreal. The three men sailed both the Weekender and their new boat for two days. It was cold, windy weather, and their little boats sailed well. By Sunday night, they agreed on the best cut and structure of the sail, the preferred mast material, and the most advantageous position and rake (angle) of the mast.

That night, at a yacht club party, they celebrated their boat's success and wondered about a better name for it. They had never really liked Weekender, which they had just chosen for the Teacup. For a month, they had been looking for inspiration in dictionaries and a thesaurus, but they hadn't found a name they liked. At the party, some university students told the sailors that they should give their boat a "modern, scientific name that

Did you know that some people enjoy sailing their Lasers in strong wind so much that there was an annual event just for them? The Laser Heavy Air Slalom was held in San Francisco Bay. Organizers planned it for what was supposed to be the windiest weekend of the summer. It takes a lot of skill to sail in high winds without toppling over.

today's youth will identify with," and Ian Bruce suggested Laser. Everyone liked it, and the next day Bruce looked up the international symbol for lasers. Fogh put that on the next sail instead of TGIF.

An International Success Story

So many people were interested in the Laser that the men knew they had to finish and protect their design before others started to copy it. Fogh searched for the highest-quality material for the sail, and Kirby and Bruce finalized the mast sections. They also filled out all the legal paperwork. One week later, Ian Bruce's company, Performance Sailcraft, began to produce Laser sailboats. The first production model went to Bruce Kirby, who still owns it today.

The second Laser was exhibited at the New York Boat Show in January 1971. It was an overnight success and 144 orders were placed for it at the boat show. Bruce Kirby

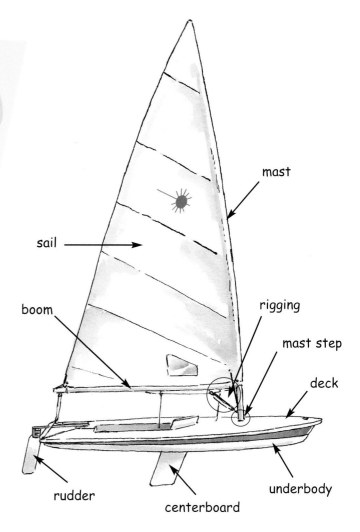

Did you know that Bruce Kirby was worried that the name Laser would not catch on because people would not know what a laser was? When his ten-year-old daughter, Kelly, arrived home from school and announced that she was learning about lasers in class, he knew they had chosen a good name for their boat.

went to work promoting the new Laser, and Performance Sailcraft sold seven hundred that first year, for $695 each.

Laser sailboats quickly became so popular worldwide that Performance Sailcraft could not build all the boats ordered. Soon other companies became licensed Laser builders. However, Performance Sailcraft wanted to control the quality of the boats internationally, so each Laser builder was made to comply with the exact specifications in a construction manual, which assures that the boats are as uniform as possible. The building method, developed by Ian Bruce, is confidential, but it takes about eight hours to make a deck in a mold, eight hours to make a hull in a mold, time to coat each one with gel and fiberglass, and then another eight hours to glue them together and assemble the fittings. Once a Laser is finished, it undergoes a quality-control check. Laser builders also buy a plaque for each boat from the International Laser Class Association; this is another way of guaranteeing quality and conformity. Each plaque attaches to the rear of the cockpit and bears its boat's sail number. If a builder

Did you know that the only changes that have been made since the first Laser was built are the addition of a compass and a few extra parts to increase the effective crew-weight range? With these alterations, lighter people can compete against their heavier rivals in strong winds.

does not meet the quality standard, he is prohibited from buying plaques and cannot sell Lasers any more.

The Laser has been called the most popular sailboat in the world. Those 144 boats first ordered have expanded to hundreds of thousands. Today Laser sailors compete in regattas worldwide, including the Olympics. Bruce Kirby, Ian Bruce, and Hans Fogh are justifiably proud of the accomplishments of the little boat that began as a piece of camping equipment.

Did you know that the serial number of a Laser sailboat is a type of code? The first three letters stand for the name of the manufacturer, the next five digits are the sail number, and the last four characters tell the month and year the Laser was built.

Glossary

awl: a sharp, smooth, pointed tool for punching holes.

bandy: an early stick-and-ball game played on ice or on grass; one of the games from which hockey evolved.

boom: a long pole that holds the bottom edge of a sail and pivots around the mast.

boxla: another name for box lacrosse, a version of lacrosse played in a space that is enclosed with boards (i.e., in a hockey rink).

crosse: the stick used in lacrosse.

ferrules: leather bands that are fitted onto a kayaker's double paddle above the blades to prevent water from running down the handle when one end of the paddle is raised and the other is dipped into the water.

foot: the lower edge of a sail; it attaches to the boom, running horizontally from the mast.

gimlet: a sharp tool used for boring holes; it looks like a screw at the tip and has a wooden handle forming a T.

gunwales: the top edge along the sides of a boat; guns were at one time supported on the gunwales.

hull: the body of a boat; the hull is the part that sits in the water.

hurley: an Irish stick-and-ball game played on grass; in North America, it was played on ice in winter and is one of the games from which hockey evolved.

join: the part of the deck that attaches to the hull of a boat.

kegling: an old-fashioned word for bowling.

loincloth: a strip of cloth worn around the hips and across the loins; roughly equivalent to a pair of shorts today.

luff: the edge of the sail that runs straight up and down the mast and faces the front of the boat.

mast: a tall, vertical pole that supports the sail.

mast step: a socket or groove that the bottom of the mast fits into.

moccasin: a handmade, soft leather shoe worn by North American Natives.

muskeg: swampy or marshy land.

neoprene: a weather-resistant synthetic rubber; it is often used to make shoe soles and snowshoe bindings.

patent: a license to use or sell an invention; prevents others from copying an idea without authorization.

pinboys: boys or young men whose job it was to set up the pins used in bowling; pinboys have been replaced by automatic pinsetters.

pitch hole: the beginning of the snowsnake track; throwers pitch snowsnakes into the wide opening, and the pitch hole narrows to guide the snakes to the thin track.

propulsion: the force that moves something forward.

prototype: the first model of something; a prototype is built and tested to see whether the design works properly.

rawhide: untanned animal skin; skin that has not been treated to be turned into leather.

rig: the top part of a boat; the rig is made up of the mast, the sail, and the ropes.

rudder: a hinged piece that hangs vertically in the water at the stern (back of a boat) and is moved to steer the boat.

shaman: a holy man believed to have the ability to contact the gods.

shiner: a person who carves and waxes snowsnakes; each shiner uses personal wax recipes, which are closely guarded secrets.

shinny: a stick-and-ball game originally credited to the Scottish people and also called shinty; today we call casual stick-and-ball or puck games like road hockey shinny.

suspension: in a vehicle, the suspension is a system of springs and other parts that supports the body and absorbs shock as the vehicle moves; it's the suspension system that allows a smooth ride.

tallow: a waxy substance made from animal fat and used for making candles and soap.

thongs: strips of leather or animal hide that were used like laces.

tramp: a group hike on snowshoes.

waterline: the place the water's surface rises to along a boat's hull; it is measured as a line running from the bow, or front of the boat, to the stern, or back.

whipper-in: the experienced snowshoer at the end of the group who helps others and makes sure that no one falls behind.

winch: a hoisting or lifting machine with a rope or chain that winds around a drum as a load is lifted.

Index

Acknowledgments

We thank everyone who helped us by pointing us in the right direction, providing information, or speaking with us, sometimes at great length. We'd particularly like to acknowledge the many librarians and archivists we consulted across Canada; Edward R. Grenda, for giving of his time and expertise in snowshoeing, snowsnake, and hockey; J. W. "Bill" Fitsell and Dale Morrisey, the International Ice Hockey Federation Museum in Kingston, Ontario; the Society for International Hockey Research; Tom Sweet, the Nova Scotia Sport Hall of Fame; Winnie Jacobs, the Woodland Cultural Centre; Kevin Jepson, the Canadian 5 Pin Bowlers' Association; Marie Gendron, the Canadian Yachting Association; Michelle Robinson and Christopher Martin Flood, the Museum and Archive of Games at the University of Waterloo; Barbara Seeber; Peggy Hooke; Julia Peterson; Andrew, Benjamin, and Rebecca Peterson; Kathy Lowinger; and our editor, Janice Weaver. A special thank-you to our families and friends for their cheerful encouragement during the research and writing of this book.